Corporate Acquisitions and Mergers in the Slovak Republic

Corporate Acquisitions and Mergers in the Slovak Republic

Adam Hodoň
Michal Hrušovský
Vladimír Polička
Tomáš Melišek
Vladimír Šimkovic

Kinstellar Bratislava

This book was originally published as a chapter in Corporate Acquisitions and Mergers.

General Editor: Peter Begg

Wolters Kluwer

Published by:
Kluwer Law International B.V.
PO Box 316
2400 AH Alphen aan den Rijn
The Netherlands
E-mail: international-sales@wolterskluwer.com
Website: lrus.wolterskluwer.com

Sold and distributed in North, Central and South America by:
Wolters Kluwer Legal & Regulatory U.S.
7201 McKinney Circle
Frederick, MD 21704
United States of America
Email: customer.service@wolterskluwer.com

Sold and distributed in all other countries by:
Air Business Subscriptions
Rockwood House
Haywards Heath
West Sussex
RH16 3DH
United Kingdom
Email: international-customerservice@wolterskluwer.com

Printed on acid-free paper

ISBN 978-94-035-1750-6

e-Book: ISBN 978-94-035-1801-5
web-PDF: ISBN 978-94-035-1845-9

This title is available on www.kluwerlawonline.com

Printed in the United Kingdom.

KINSTELLAR BRATISLAVA

Kinstellar is a leading independent law firm in Emerging Europe, Turkey and Central Asia, with offices in Almaty and Nur-Sultan (Kazakhstan), Belgrade (Serbia), Bratislava (Slovakia), Bucharest (Romania), Budapest (Hungary), Istanbul (Turkey), Kyiv (Ukraine), Prague (the Czech Republic), Sofia (Bulgaria) and Tashkent (Uzbekistan).

Operating as a single fully-integrated firm, Kinstellar delivers consistently high-quality services across all jurisdictions in an integrated and seamless style. We are particularly well suited to servicing complex transactions and advisory requirements spanning several jurisdictions. With offices in ten jurisdictions and over 200 local and international lawyers, we deliver consistent, joined-up legal advice and assistance across diverse regional markets.

Our clients include leading international and regional corporations, banks and other financial institutions, state bodies, multi-lateral institutions, and international law firms with clients that require top-quality legal counsel in our jurisdictions. We handle the most important and complex assignments for clients across diverse industries and business sectors.

Kinstellar covers all aspects of domestic and international law, including Banking, Finance and Capital Markets, Competition and State Aid, Compliance, Risk and Sensitive Investigations, Dispute Resolution, Employment and Labour Law, Energy, Infrastructure and Projects, Intellectual Property, Life Sciences and Healthcare, M&A and Corporate, Private Equity, Real Estate, Restructuring and Insolvency, Tax, Telecoms, Media and Technology.

Authors

This country chapter on Corporate M&A in Slovakia has been written by the following team of lawyers of Kinstellar Bratislava: Adam Hodoň (Partner) – *Local economic, political and cultural aspects*, Michal Hrušovský (Senior Associate) – *The regulatory framework*, Michal Hrušovský (Senior Associate) – *Laws affecting M&A*; *Controls/Restrictions on Foreign Investment*, Adam Hodoň (Partner) – *Incentives for foreign investment*, Vladimír Polička (Managing Associate) – *Specific issues of company/ securities law*, Tomáš Melišek (Managing Associate) – *Insolvency*, Michal Hrušovský (Senior Associate) – *Choice of Law*, Vladimír Polička (Managing Associate) – *Specific Rules on Public Takeovers*, Michal Hrušovský (Senior Associate) – *Other relevant laws*, Tomáš Melišek (Managing Associate) – *The due diligence process*, Michal Hrušovský (Senior Associate) – *Role of the Courts*, Vladimír Šimkovic (Associate) – *Merger Control*, Adam Hodoň (Partner) – *Taxation*, *Employment Considerations* and *Accounting treatment*.

The chapter has been reviewed and coordinated by Adam Hodoň, Partner in the Bratislava office.

Kinstellar, s.r.o.

Hviezdoslavovo námestie 13

811 02 Bratislava

Slovak Republic

Tel.: (421 2) 5929 1111

Fax: (421 2) 5929 1210

Web: www.kinstellar.com

Disclaimer

This document does not purport to contain a comprehensive summary of all the legal risks and issues in the legal areas it covers. It is to be used for information only and cannot be relied upon as legal advice, no legal or business decision should be based solely on this document.

Contents

LOCAL ECONOMIC, POLITICAL AND CULTURAL ASPECTS

General Comments on the Country Profile

[01] The Slovak Republic (further also '**Slovakia**') lies at the intersection of Western and Eastern Europe and has very tight historical, political, cultural, economic and commercial ties with its neighbouring countries – the Czech Republic, Poland, Hungary, Austria and, to a lesser extent, Ukraine. The total population of Slovakia is about 5 415 000 people. The capital city is Bratislava, with a population of about 600 000. The official language is Slovak and the currency is the Euro.

[02] The recent history of Slovak Republic began in 1918 when the Republic of Czechoslovakia was formed. During the Second World War, the two countries briefly split and fell under German occupation, only to be joined again after the Second World War, which was also marked with the coming of the Soviet influence in 1948, resulting in a single-party communist state. Eventually, a period of liberalization started to emerge, which was stopped by the occupation of Warsaw Pact forces in 1968. Czechoslovakia remained occupied until 1989 when the Velvet Revolution overthrew the communist regime. On 1 January 1993, Czechoslovakia peacefully split into two separate states, the Slovak Republic and the Czech Republic.

[03] The period following the Velvet Revolution was marked with political changes, economic reforms and extensive privatization, resulting in a modern, free-market driven economy. Slovakia became a member of North Atlantic Treaty Organization (NATO) on 29 March 2004 and of the European Union (EU) on 1 May 2004. On 1 January 2009, Slovakia adopted the Euro as its national currency and thus replaced its previous currency, the Slovak crown. Since 2007, Slovakia has formed a part of the Schengen Area.

[04] Slovakia is divided into eight separate administrative divisions and each one is further subdivided into districts. Transport in Slovakia is possible by road, rail, air or river. While Slovakia has a well-developed rail network of roughly 3 600 km, the highway system is still rather underdeveloped (approximately 400 km of highways and 200 km of expressways) and is considered to be one of the weaknesses of Slovak infrastructure. It is expected that the capital Bratislava (located in south-west of the country, 60 km from Vienna) will be connected with the eastern regions (dominated by the city of Košice) by the end of 2020.

Government and Political System

[05] Slovakia is a member of the EU since 2004 and of the Eurozone since 2009. It is also member of NATO, World Trade Organization (WTO), The Organization for Security and Co-operation in Europe (OSCE) and a number of other international organizations, which make the country a fully integrated West-European-style and stable state, with few specifics typical for countries of the former Soviet block in Central and Eastern Europe (CEE).

[06] Slovakia is a parliamentary representative democratic republic with a multi-party system. The legislative power is vested in the parliament, while the executive is performed by the government, which is led by the Prime Minister. As of 2019, the leading party is *Smer – Social Democracy*, with 32% of the seats. There are seven other political parties in the parliament. While *Smer – Social Democracy*, representing the left-wing politics, is usually stable, the right-wing parties have had troubles in the past to find common ground. Next parliamentary elections are scheduled for March 2020. The president is the formal head of the state, albeit with limited powers.

Legal System

[07] While in the aftermath of the 1989 Velvet Revolution, which toppled the Communist regime in Czechoslovakia, the new democracy remodelled much of its post-Communist legislation on German and Austrian laws and traditions, the legislation today is very much driven by the European law. Legislation and important case law in this section reflect the situation as of 1 January 2019.

[08] Business people and legal practitioners who are used to working in civil law jurisdictions will not feel ill-at-ease with the structure of the commercial law in the Slovak Republic. There are certainly many features in the Slovak legal system that are particular to this country, but the framework will be familiar. These features and the system itself will seem quite different to business people and lawyers accustomed to a common law environment.

[09] In many aspects, the Slovak legal environment is liberal, with few impediments to, and legislated protection of, foreign investments. However, unlike in most common law jurisdictions and some civil law jurisdictions, many transactions are governed by unalterable rules. While parties are free, within the framework of the law, to determine the terms and conditions of the contracts into which they enter, this framework gives the parties little room to manoeuvre. Contributing to this is the fact that, in the majority of cases, courts and some practitioners still interpret the Slovak law in a formalistic manner.

[10] Parties to contracts in Slovakia are free to decide whether to use the general courts of law or arbitration proceedings to resolve any disputes that may arise between them, unless the dispute falls within the exclusive jurisdiction of courts (e.g., title to real estate). Unless the agreement stipulates otherwise, territorial jurisdiction of the court is governed by applicable legal regulations or international private law. However, it is worth noting that obtaining effective legal protection in front of Slovak courts is one of the well-recognized problems of the Slovak judicial system. Slowness and inefficiency often lead to corruption of the judiciary. Therefore, in many cases, it is advisable/worthwhile to opt for an alternative dispute resolution.

Current Economic Aspects

[11] The Slovak economy has been nicknamed the 'Tatra Tiger' in the past, reflecting its rapid growth. In 2007 Slovakia had the highest sustained Gross Domestic Product (GDP) growth in the EU, which resulted in a considerable lowering of unemployment. Following the economic crisis, the GDP development was halted, however as of 2013 it is on the rise again, and continues to grow at the robust rate (3.4 % in 2017, 3.3 % in 2018 and predictions show 3.7% in the *1st* quarter of 2019), being one of the fastest-growing economies in the EU.

[12] The unemployment rate has reduced significantly to around 5.8% at the beginning of 2019. As it becomes apparent in 2018 and 2019, many employers actually face new issue never experienced before in Slovakia: lack of skilled labour.

[13] After gaining its independence in 1993, Slovakia presented an attractive destination for investment, which was slowed down by poor reforms. Nowadays, the Slovak economy is very open and, as such, largely based on foreign direct investment (FDI), resulting in a relatively investor-friendly environment, with an 'ease of doing business' index of 42 (out of 190 economies).[1] Generally, Slovakia is perceived as investor-friendly, with attractive tax laws. Foreign Direct InvestmentFDI has increased by 600% since 2000 and the country is still seeking to provide incentives for investment, although not to such wide extent as in the past.

[14] Given the relatively small market, there is very little separate statistics on M&A deal volumes for Slovakia as such. Slovakia is reported as an integral part of the CEE region, which itself is being consistently described as the fastest growing and most interesting markets for M&A in Europe.

Main Industries

[15] There is no institutionalized protection of Slovak industries against foreign ownership (save for certain limitations on purchase of agricultural land by foreigners). In fact, many of the largest Slovak businesses (including banks and other financial institutions) are either fully or partially owned by foreign shareholders. Since the late nineties to date, Slovak government has also privatized most 'strategic' state-owned companies including Slovak Telekom (to Deutsche Telekom), Slovak electricity generation company (to ENEL – currently in different hands), electricity distribution companies (to E.ON, EdF, RWE) and most Slovak banks (e.g. to Raiffeisen, Erste, KBC and Intesa). In some of these companies, the Slovak government retained either minority share, or majority (usually 50% + 1) share while conferring management control to foreign investors.

[16] While the privatizations and private sales in the late nineties and in the first decade of *twenty-first* century saw most strategic buyers, in the recent years financial

[1] http://www.doingbusiness.org/data/exploreeconomies/slovakia/.

investors become important. For example, some of the gas and electricity distribution assets have been acquired from the original strategic investors by Czech- and Slovak- based financial investors and private equity groups (PPF, EPH/J&T) and similar deals with large private equity buyers are seen more frequently since 2010.

[17] Nowadays, the Slovak industry is based on a highly skilled workforce, mainly in automotive, informational technology, electronics, mechanical engineering and chemical engineering. Especially the automotive industry presents a main pillar of Slovak industry. Due to the large investments of Volkswagen, PSA – Peugeot, Kia Motors and most recently Jaguar Land Rover (which opened its production facility in Western Slovakia in 2018), Slovakia is one of the leading car producers in the world and the world leader in car production per capita.

[18] It is also worth noting, that recently many companies have emerged on the market with a higher added value and knowledge-based economy. This has resulted in many companies being established, aiding local research and development, such as Dell, Capco, Amazon or the Kosice IT valley – an association of companies and educational institutions, aiding IT development in eastern Slovakia.

[19] Among the top companies functioning in Slovakia are VOLKSWAGEN SLOVAKIA, SLOVNAFT, Kia Motors Slovakia, SAMSUNG Electronics Slovakia, Slovenske elektrarne and U.S. Steel Kosice.

Cultural Aspects

[20] Throughout most of its history, Slovakia has been part of a larger entity (Kingdom of Hungary, Austro – Hungarian monarchy, Czechoslovakia, Soviet block, now the EU). This has several cultural implications: on one hand, one can sense somewhat unconstructive feelings towards the former 'oppressors', 'rulers' and a 'older brother complex' towards some nationalities (these however seem to fade away over time). On the other hand, there has always been very tight cooperation, communication, trading and all sorts of business and cultural relationships with all neighbours of the country, which is reflected in an open and friendly attitude towards foreign investment. The generation of Slovaks born until the 1950' in the region of Bratislava commonly spoke German and/or Hungarian. Russian was the preferred language in the education system in the communist era, and English becomes a natural second language of young generation born after 1990 (many will at the same time speak German, Spanish or French). These factors create favourable conditions for doing businesses by foreigners in Slovakia.

[21] Due to the fact that Slovakia is largely influenced by Western-style culture, business practices should not present a hurdle for foreigners. At first, the people tend to be quiet and reserved, although this is not always the rule. The Slovaks differentiate between formal and informal speech. Business relations tend to be led in a formal tone, which may appear cold at first. For this reason, it is polite to wait to be invited before using someone's first name. It is generally advisable, to let the partner set the tone of communication. Business cards are usually exchanged without any rituals. Business meetings and lunches are common, being invited to someone's home is more rare. In such a case, it is customary to bring a gift, such as flowers or a bottle of wine.

THE REGULATORY FRAMEWORK

Forms of Doing Business

[22] Business in Slovakia may be conducted by a variety of entrepreneurial entities. These include entrepreneurs carrying out business alone (sole traders) and the following types of companies:

(i) limited liability companies (*spoločnosť s ručením obmedzeným* or *s.r.o.*);
(ii) joint-stock companies (*akciová spoločnosť* or *a.s.*);
(iii) simplified joint-stock companies (*jednoduchá spoločnosť* na akcie or *j.s.a.*);
(iv) general commercial partnerships (*verejná obchodná spoločnosť* or *v.o.s.*); and
(v) limited partnerships (*komanditná spoločnosť* or *k.s.*).

Cooperatives (*družstvo*) also exist as a special legal form.

[23] Generally, foreign entities can register to conduct business in the Slovak Republic via a branch or through participation in Slovak entities under the same conditions as the Slovak entities. In addition, the following European forms of legal entities are allowed to operate in the Slovak Republic:

(i) European Economic Interest Grouping.
(ii) European Company (Societas Europea); and
(iii) European Cooperative Society.

[24] Within the context of corporate mergers and acquisitions, it is primarily limited liability companies and joint-stock companies that are involved. Both are equity-based and have registered capital that is contributed by their founders. They are both distinct legal entities, and the financial responsibility of their shareholders is limited.

[25] Generally, both individuals and legal entities may become a shareholder in a limited liability or joint-stock company. As far as sole ownership is concerned, generally both a limited liability company and a joint-stock company may have a sole owner and both may be the sole owner of another company. Thus, for example, a limited liability company may become the sole shareholder of a joint-stock company, or vice versa. Other types of entrepreneurial entities may also become the sole owner of a joint-stock company or a limited liability company. Furthermore, two or more companies may be merged or consolidated into one company without liquidation of the companies.

Commercial Register

[26] All types of companies and cooperatives are legal entities and are registered in the Commercial Register kept by the District Court located in the seat of the region where the company has its registered office (the '*Commercial Register*'). With registration in the Commercial Register, which takes up to two business days from filing an application, a company comes into existence and may commence to carry out its business activities. In addition, any change to details registered in the Commercial Register, such as the business name or registered office, must be registered within thirty days after the day of the decision of the shareholders or other body of the company on such change. In most cases, the registration of new facts in the Commercial Register is of a declaratory nature; that is, change is effective irrespective of registration (except, for example, for change of the business name, registered office or change in majority shareholder, where the registration is of a constitutive nature; that is, such change will become effective *vis-á-vis* third parties only upon registration in the Commercial Register).

[27] In principle, if a third party relies on information registered in the Commercial Register, it is protected against the registered entity in the event that information is proved to be untrue unless the registered entity proves that the third party was aware of such fact. The Commercial Register is also accessible through its online database on the Internet at *www.orsr.sk*. Although the online database of the Commercial Register is in general reliable, the information should be verified by original (hard copy) extract from the Commercial Register, as that is the only official source of information about a company that can be used for legal purposes.

[28] The Commercial Register maintains a collection of deeds, in which the important corporate documents, such as founding deeds, memoranda of association, articles of association and financial statements, are deposited (the '*Collection of Deeds*'), and the documents deposited there are accessible to the public.[2] Most of the documents (except, for example, for the financial statements, which must be filed in electronic form through tax administration) are to be deposited in the Collection of Deeds as original or a copy verified by notary.

[29] All types of documents that are to be submitted to the Commercial Register and the Collection of Deeds must be either executed in Slovak or may be executed in a foreign language and translated into Slovak by a sworn Slovak translator.

[2] The list of documents (but not the documents as such) deposited in the Collection of Deeds can be accessed electronically (online). The access is free. Hard copy of the documents can be obtained from the Collection of Deeds upon a written request and the payment of an administration fee. An electronic copy can be also requested through an online governmental portal subject to payment of administration fee.

Limited Liability Company

Basic Characteristics

[30] A limited liability company (*spoločnosť s ručením obmedzeným* or *s.r.o.* or *spol. s r.o.*) is the vehicle generally preferred by enterprises with a limited number of investors who plan to hold their investments in the company for the mid- to long-term. A limited liability company is typically used by small to medium-size enterprises. The regulation of a limited liability company is very liberal and gives shareholders great freedom to change their rights and obligations *vis-á-vis* each other and the company.

Founding

[31] A limited liability company may be founded by one shareholder, either an individual or a legal entity, and it may have a maximum of fifty shareholders.

[32] A limited liability company with a sole shareholder shall neither be the sole founder nor the sole shareholder of another limited liability company. One individual shall not be a sole shareholder of more than three limited liability companies. Although it is not clear under the Slovak law whether these restrictions apply also to foreign entities, that is, whether a foreign entity with a sole shareholder may be the sole founder or the sole shareholder of a limited liability company (the so-called anti-chaining rule), the prevailing view of the leading Slovak practitioners is that these restrictions also apply to foreign limited liability companies.

[33] The founders establish a company by execution of a memorandum of association or, in the case of a sole shareholder, a founding deed. However, the company is created only after it has been duly registered with the Commercial Register and only then it may commence to carry out its business activities.

Registered Capital

[34] The registered capital of a limited liability company is composed of the contributions made by the shareholders. The minimum amount of registered capital for a limited liability company is EUR5 000. The minimum contribution by one shareholder to the registered capital is EUR750.

[35] The registered capital of a limited liability company and the capital contributions of individual shareholders are recorded in the Commercial Register. Any changes to the registered capital must be approved by the general meeting and recorded in the Commercial Register. Contributions to the registered capital of a limited liability company can be either cash or in-kind; the value of in-kind contributions must be determined by independent expert. An enterprise or its part or a receivable may be also contributed to the company's registered capital.

[36] Non-monetary contributions must be fully paid before the company's registration in the Commercial Register. The founder's deed or memorandum of association must specify the non-monetary contribution and its value. At least 30% (100% if there is only one founder) of subscribed monetary contributions must be paid up before the registration of the company in the Commercial Register.

[37] Registered capital of a limited liability company is divided in ownership interests (*obchodný podiel*).

Ownership Interest

[38] A limited liability company does not issue shares. The ownership interest represents the shareholder's participation in the company and the rights and duties derived from such participation. The size of the ownership interest is determined by the ratio of a particular shareholder's investment contribution to the company's registered capital. The memorandum of association may set out ownership interests that differ from interests calculated based on shareholders' contributions. Each shareholder may only hold one ownership interest. Co-ownership of ownership interest in a limited liability company is possible.

[39] Shareholders are personally liable, jointly and severally, for the obligations of the company equivalent to the sum of the unpaid capital contributions as registered in the Commercial Register. The shareholders' liability terminates upon full repayment of all capital contributions in the Commercial Register.

[40] Shareholders may contribute to capital fund to increase the equity of a limited liability company. Such contributions must be approved by the general meeting, but no registration in the Commercial Register is required. Besides this voluntary contribution to capital fund, if set out by the memorandum of association, the general meeting may approve a decision obliging shareholders to contribute to the equity of the limited liability company.

Transfer of Ownership Interest

[41] An ownership interest in a limited liability company is not as easily transferable as the shares in a joint-stock company. It requires a written agreement (with notarized signatures). A shareholder may transfer his ownership interest to another shareholder only with the approval of the general meeting (however, the memorandum of association may stipulate no such approval is required). A shareholder may transfer his ownership interest to a third party only if such transfer is allowed by the memorandum of association. Also, the memorandum of association may stipulate that such transfer of ownership interest to a third party requires approval of the general meeting.

[42] Transfer of a majority ownership interest is effective only upon registration of the transfer with the Commercial Register (i.e. the registration has a constitutive character) and one of the preconditions for such transfer is a prior approval of the tax office.

[43] Transfer of minority ownership interest is effective upon delivery of the agreement on transfer of ownership interest to the company and no approval of the tax office is required.

Acting on Behalf of a Limited Liability Company

[44] A limited liability company is represented by one or more executive directors (*konatel*). Unless the memorandum of association stipulates otherwise, each executive director may act independently. Information on whether an executive director may act independently or whether the memorandum of association requires executive directors to act jointly must be registered in the Commercial Register.

[45] The relationship between the executive directors and the company is governed by the Commercial Code and can be based on an agreement on discharge of the office concluded under the Commercial Code). The relationship between the executive director and the company shall not be of employment nature.

[46] Commercial management of a limited liability company falls within the powers of executive directors and, if there is more than one executive director, the management decisions are taken by majority of them, unless the memorandum of association specifies otherwise. The shareholders are entitled to demand information from its executive director(s) about the affairs of a limited liability company and to inspect all of the company's documents, including its financial statements.

Duty of Care

[47] Executive directors must act with the care of a diligent manager and their responsibility cannot be limited or excluded. In the course of carrying out their tasks, they must proceed in line with interest of the company and its shareholders.

[48] When deciding on any matters relating to the company, they are obliged to obtain, and take into consideration all accessible information concerning the subject-matter of the particular decision; they are also bound by the confidentiality obligation.

[49] The executive directors who breached their duties when exercising their powers are (jointly and severally) obliged to compensate the company for any damages caused by their actions. However, an executive director will not be responsible for damages if he proves that he acted in a diligent manner and good faith; also, executive directors are not liable for damage incurred when they were implementing a decision of general meeting (unless such decision is in breach of law, articles of association of the company or memorandum of association). Liability of an executive director can be excluded neither by agreement nor by memorandum of association.

[50] Illegal acts of executive directors may also result in criminal liability of the directors, or even criminal liability of the company.

Other Important Issues

[51] Audit of financial statements is mandatory if the company meets at least two of the following criteria in the immediately preceding accounting period:

(i) value of its total assets exceeds EUR1 m;
(ii) annual net turnover exceeds EUR2 m; and/or
(iii) its average number of employees is more than thirty.

[52] Reserve fund is obligatory. If not created at the time of establishment, then it must be created in the amount equal to 5% of the net profit in the year in which the company recorded profit for the first time. It must be regularly replenished until equivalent to at least 10% of the registered capital or to such higher amount set out in the memorandum of association. The reserve fund representing the minimal amount required by law may only be used to cover the company's losses.

[53] A limited liability company may, but is not required to, have a supervisory board. If a supervisory board exists, its position and competences are similar to the supervisory board of a joint-stock company.

Joint-Stock Company

Basic Characteristics

[54] A joint-stock company (*akciová spoločnosť* or *a.s.*) is the form of company generally used for larger businesses. It may be established as a private or public joint-stock company; shares of a public joint-stock company can be traded at a regulated market.

Founding

[55] A joint-stock company may be founded by one or more legal entities, by two or more individuals, or by a combination of individuals and legal entities. A joint-stock company may have an unlimited number of founders and an unlimited number of shareholders.

[56] The founders establish the company through execution of the founding agreement or, where there is a sole shareholder, of the founding deed, both in the form of a notarial deed. The articles of association, which are the most important corporate document of a joint-stock company, are attached to the founding document. A joint-stock company can be also founded by way of a public offer of shares. However, this is not a common practice in the Slovak Republic.

Registered Capital and Shares

[57] Registered capital of a joint-stock company is divided into shares with a specified nominal value. The minimum amount of registered capital is EUR25 000.

[58] The shares may be either registered shares (issued to a named shareholder) or bearer shares. Both registered shares and bearer shares may be issued in de-materialized form as book-entered shares registered on the shareholder's account at the Central Securities Depository (CSD) (*Centrálny depozitár cenných papierov*). Bearer shares cannot be issued solely as physical share certificates and they always must be book-entered. Registered shares may also be 'certificated', that is to say, physical share certificates are issued to a registered shareholder.

[59] In addition, certificated shares can be issued individually or they can be issued in the form of global share certificate which replaces a certain number 'of certificated shares'.

[60] Generally, all of the company's shareholders must be treated equally by the company. However, shares of different classes, both common and preferred, may be issued if the articles of association provide for multiple classes of shares and describe the rights attached to such different classes of shares. Identical rights must be attached to all shares of a given class. Total nominal value of preferred shares must not exceed one-half of the company's registered capital. No special rights are attached to common shares. Preferred shares may have a priority right to dividends and to any liquidation surplus attached to them.

[61] The amount of registered capital of a joint-stock company and the information about the issued shares are recorded in the Commercial Register. Any changes to the registered capital or to shares must be approved by the general meeting in the form of a notarial deed and recorded in the Commercial Register. Generally, an increase in registered capital is deemed to be effective as of the date of registration of the increased amount in the Commercial Register (unless the registered capital is increased by the board of directors authorized by the general meeting, in which case the increase is effective once the nominal value of all shares subscribed for the increase of registered capital has been paid up).

[62] Contributions to the registered capital of a joint-stock company can be either cash or in-kind. The value of any in-kind contributions must be determined by an independent expert and paid up before the registration of the registered capital in the Commercial Register.

Acting on Behalf of a Joint-Stock Company

[63] A joint-stock company is represented and managed by its board of directors. The board of directors makes decisions on behalf of the company on all matters relating to the company, unless such matters are reserved to the general meeting or supervisory board by law or articles of association.

[64] The composition of the board of directors is determined by the articles of association; the minimum number of the board members is one.

[65] Unless the articles of association state otherwise, each member of the board of directors may independently perform legal acts that are binding on the joint-stock company. Information on whether a member of the board of directors may act independently or whether the articles of association require members of the board of directors to act jointly must be registered in the Commercial Register. Decisions of the board of directors are taken by simple majority or other majority as specified in the articles of association. The board of directors is a 'collective' body and its decisions must be recorded in minutes.

Duty of Care

[66] Members of the board of directors must carry out their duties with due care and in accordance with interests of the company and its shareholders.

[67] When deciding on any matters relating to the company, they are obliged to obtain, and take into consideration all accessible information concerning the subject-matter of the particular decision; they are also bound by the confidentiality obligation.

[68] The board members who breached their duties when exercising their powers are (jointly and severally) obliged to compensate the company for any damages caused by their actions. However, the board member will not be responsible for damages if he proves that he acted in a diligent manner and good faith; also, board members are not liable for damage incurred when they were implementing a decision of general meeting (unless such decision is in breach of law, articles of association of the company or memorandum of association). Liability of a member of the board of directors cannot be excluded by agreement or by articles of association.

[69] Illegal acts of members of the board of directors may also result in criminal liability of the directors or even criminal liability of the company.

Other Corporate Bodies

[70] A joint-stock company must have a supervisory board, which oversees the manner in which the board of directors exercises its powers and the manner in which the business of the joint-stock company is conducted. For this purpose, the supervisory board has the right to examine all the records and documents of the joint-stock company (including its financial statements, minutes of the board of directors, etc.). The supervisory board also has the right to convene a general meeting of shareholders if the company's interests require so; it may also represent the joint-stock company in actions against members of the board of directors. Members of the supervisory board must act with the care of a diligent manager. Only an individual (i.e. not a business company) may be a member of the supervisory board and his or her office is incompatible with that of a member of the board of directors.

[71] The supervisory board must have at least three members and, if the joint-stock company has more than fifty full-time employees, one-third of the supervisory board members are elected by the employees.

[72] Entities of public interest (i.e., in particular banks and insurance companies) must establish an audit committee as another mandatory body of a joint-stock company.

Shareholders' Rights

[73] At the general meeting, shareholders are entitled to inspect and approve the financial statements of a joint-stock company and the reports prepared by the board of directors and the supervisory board.

[74] Shareholders may appoint and recall members of the board of directors (unless the articles of association stipulate that the supervisory board appoint the members of the board of directors) and the members of the supervisory board, with the exception of those members of the supervisory board elected by employees.

[75] Shareholders may also vote on certain key issues specified in the articles of association relating to the joint-stock company, but they are not allowed to give instructions to the board of directors regarding the management of the company.

[76] No shareholder is entitled to receive any business-related information from the management of a company other than the reports and other information provided to all shareholders.

[77] Shareholders participate in the profits of the joint-stock company through dividends approved by the general meeting of shareholders. Neither the articles of association nor the general meeting can restrict or exclude the shareholder's right to receive dividends. Dividends may only be paid if the general meeting has approved the payout on the basis of the company's performance as set out in the annual statement, and upon the fulfilment of the mandatory obligations for the payout of dividends under the Commercial Code. The law explicitly prohibits dividend prepayments ('interim dividends') before the general meeting has decided to pay dividends. In addition, the right to receive dividends can only be transferred separately after the decision of the general meeting on dividends has been taken. The basis for the payment of dividends are the financial results of the company for the previous accounting period(s) – the distributable amount is not just the profit shown in the last annual statement, but also undistributed profit from previous years or other funds which have been accumulated from profits, unless the use of such funds is limited to certain purposes. The amount of the profit which can be distributed is based on the profit less obligatory payments to reserve funds and less uncovered losses from previous years. A company must not distribute profit to its shareholders if such profit distribution might cause the equity to fall below the amount of the registered capital.

[78] Under the Commercial Code, all shareholders must be treated equally. Minority shareholders holding shares with the nominal value amounting to at least 5% of the registered capital may request that the board of directors convene a general meeting with an agenda proposed by the minority shareholders. Each shareholder is also generally entitled to challenge a decision of the general meeting in court.

[79] If the joint-stock company is to increase its registered capital by cash contributions, all shareholders have a pre-emptive right to subscribe to newly issued shares, which may be limited or excluded by a decision of the general meeting only (i) if it is in an urgent interest of the company recognized by the general meeting or (ii) if

it is required by law. In the scenario (i), the board of directors must present the general meeting with a written report reasoning the proposal for limitation or exclusion of the pre-emptive right.

Other Important Issues

[80] Audit of the financial statements is mandatory if a joint-stock company meets at least two of the following three criteria for the immediately preceding accounting period:

(i) value of its total assets exceeds EUR1 m;
(ii) annual net turnover exceeds EUR2 m; and/or
(iii) the average number of employees exceeds 30.

[81] Reserve fund totalling 10% of the registered capital is obligatory at the time of incorporation. It must be replenished each year by an amount determined in the articles of association, and in any case by at least 10% of the net profit declared in the financial statements, until the reserve fund reaches 20% of the registered capital. The reserve fund may be used only for covering the company's losses.

Simplified Joint-Stock Company

Basic Characteristics

[82] A simplified joint-stock company (*jednoduchá spoločnosť'* na akcie or *j.s.a.*) is a relatively new form of company (available from 2017) intended to be used for smaller and flexible businesses with potential to grow (start-ups). It may also turn out to be the best company form for venture capital deals and for PE investments involving less than 100% equity (both minority and majority buy-outs).

[83] The basics of corporate governance are identical with the joint stock company as described under paragraph **[54]–[81]** above.

Unique Features of j.s.a.

[84] As its most significant advantage, all internal relations between shareholders, stakeholders and business owners can be set with unparalleled freedom. Mainly, this can be achieved through company's shares, which the shareholders are free to issue in various classes, entitling to a wide range of rights. There are no explicit limitations on rights that can be attached to shares in the company; thus, shareholders can create various shareholder classes that reflect their position or time when they entered the company. Unlike the other forms of capital companies in Slovakia, the j.s.a. will make it possible to issue 'employee shares' which can prove to be very efficient for employee motivation and reward.

[85] This company form also brings an explicit acknowledgement and use of standard investor tools, in particular, (i) drag-along right, (ii) tag-along right and (iii) deadlock mechanism (shoot-out). All of these (and other) mechanisms can be agreed in shareholders' agreement and enjoy legal protection. In addition, these contractual rights can be registered in a special public register, in a way similar to registration of pledge. Upon registration, such rights can be then enforced very quickly – within few weeks or months, as opposed to substantially longer periods that court or arbitration proceedings may take.

[86] The j.s.a. can be founded only as a private company and its minimum registered capital is EUR1.

[87] The j.s.a. may (but does not need to) form the supervisory board.

Partnerships

[88] Partnerships are not commonly used as business vehicles in Slovakia. However, operating business in form of a partnership might sometimes be justified by tax-related reasons; this is, for example, due to favourable classification of the partnership in some double taxation treaties to which Slovakia is a party, and due to flow-through taxation of partnerships under Slovak legislation.

General Partnership (*verejná obchodná spoločnosť or v.o.s.*)

[89] A general partnership is a legal entity formed by a partnership agreement, in which at least two persons (natural individuals or legal entities) carry out business activities under a common commercial name and bear joint and several liability for the partnership's obligations with all their property. Each partner can only have a single investment contribution in the partnership.

[90] Conducting business in the form of general partnership has the following benefits:

(i) the Commercial Code does not stipulate the obligation to create registered capital or the obligation of the partners to invest a contribution in the partnership;
(ii) the partnership requires no special bodies (general meeting, supervisory board);
(iii) maintenance of single entry bookkeeping; the financial statements of the partnership do not need to be reviewed by an auditor.

[91] Disadvantage is in liability – the partnership is liable for its obligations by its entire property; partners have joint and several liability for the partnership's obligations with their entire property.

Limited Partnership (*komanditná spoločnosť or k.s.*)

[92] A limited partnership is a hybrid half-way between a general partnership and a limited liability company. It is a legal entity formed by a partnership agreement, in which one or more partners are liable for the partnership's obligation up to the amount of the unpaid parts of their contributions, as recorded in the Commercial Code ('limited partners') and one or more partners are liable for the partnership's obligations with their entire property ('general partners'). Therefore, it means that the liability of the limited partners is limited by the amount of their paid-up contributions recorded in the Commercial Code and thus limited partners are liable for the partnership's obligations only until the moment when it is recorded in the Commercial Code that they paid up the entire contribution.

[93] The limited partner is obliged to invest a contribution in the registered capital of the partnership in the amount specified by the partnership agreement, however, EUR250 is the minimum. Advantages include:

(i) Formation is not demanding in terms of capital – the law does not stipulate a minimum obligatory amount of registered capital, only a minimum investment contribution of the limited partner is specified to at least EUR250).
(ii) The partnership requires no special bodies (general meeting, supervisory board).

[94] The partnership is liable for its obligations by its entire property; general partners are liable for partnership's obligations with their entire property, similarly to the partners of a general partnership; limited partners are liable up to the amount of their unpaid investment contribution as recorded in the Commercial Register.

LAWS AFFECTING M&A

Regulatory Framework

[95] There is no particular legislation which would specifically regulate the M&A practice in all its aspects. In general, both types – private and public M&A – are regulated by the:

- Act No. 513/1991 Coll., the Commercial Code, as amended (the '**Commercial Code**').
- Act No. 40/1964 Coll., the Civil Code, as amended; and
- Act No. 566/2001 Coll., on Securities and Investment Services, as amended (the '**Securities Act'**) in respect of the public M&A transactions.

[96] Furthermore, M&A activities in relation to regulated businesses such as banks, insurance companies, investment firms are subject to additional regulations. Accordingly, the following laws may be applicable:

- Act No. 483/2001 Coll., on Banks and Amendment of Certain Other Laws, as amended (the '**Banking Act**').
- Act No. 566/1992 Coll. on National Bank of Slovakia, as amended (the '**Act on National Bank of Slovakia**').

- Act No. 202/1995 Coll., the Foreign Exchange Act, as amended (the '**Foreign Exchange Act**').
- Act No. 39/2015 Coll., on Insurance and Amendment of Certain Other Laws, as amended.
- Act No. 203/2011 Coll., on Collective Investment, as amended.
- Act No. 429/2002 Coll., on Stock Exchange, as amended.
- Act No. 43/2004 Coll., on Retirement Pension Insurance and Amendment of Certain Other Laws, as amended.
- Act No. 650/2004 Coll., on Supplementary Pension Insurance and Amendment of Certain Other Laws, as amended.

[97] In addition, to the general laws and specific laws relating to regulated entities, the M&A activity is typically affected by the following laws:

- Act No. 431/2002 Coll. on Accountancy, as amended (the '**Accountancy Act**').
- Act No. 455/1991 Coll., on Trades Licensing, as amended (the '**Trades Licensing Act**').
- Act No. 136/2001 Coll., on Protection of Economic Competition and Organisation of Ministries and Other State Departments, as amended.
- Act No. 7/2005 Coll., on Bankruptcy and Restructuring, as amended (the '**Insolvency Code**').

[98] In essence, the law is flexible and parties are generally free to agree contractual arrangements regarding their M&A transactions. Certain limitations nonetheless apply; for instance future waiver of rights is not enforceable as a matter of Slovak law.

[99] Given the undeveloped capital markets in Slovakia, public deals are virtually non-existent and the M&A activity remains exclusively in the private domain. In practice, consequently, there are no differences between the friendly and hostile takeovers.

[100] There are no voluntary codes (equivalent to the United Kingdom (UK) Takeover Code or the like) nor self-regulation mechanisms in place that would regulate M&A activities in Slovakia. In addition, there are no self-regulating bodies that would oversee the conduct of M&A activities and such regulation and oversight are left to state/government regulatory authorities (*see* further below).

Relevant Regulatory Authorities

General

[101] There are only few governmental/regulatory authorities in Slovakia that are relevant to the M&A transactions.

[102] In principle, no regulatory approvals in respect of M&A transactions are required save for certain narrow exceptions provided for regulated entities. The regulated entities for which a regulatory consent is typically required in connection with M&A are exclusively entities within the financial services markets (such as banks, insurance companies, investment firms).

[103] Regulatory approvals in the M&A context are also required for public takeovers, however in the absence of public companies in Slovakia, its practical application is rather limited.

[104] In addition, regarding M&A transactions that meet the notification criteria, the usual competition/antitrust clearances also apply in respect to all types of companies (*see* further paragraph **[349]–[386]**).

[105] While it is possible to engage personally/proactively with regulatory authorities, it is customary that the proceedings concerning M&A transactions before the governmental/regulatory authorities are handled through advisers.

Financial Authorities

[106] The National Bank of Slovakia is the only regulator and supervisor of the financial markets (including the securities markets). In particular, the National Bank of Slovakia has the prudential powers over the following areas:

- banking industry supervision;
- securities market supervision;
- payment institutions supervision;
- electronic money institutions supervision;
- insurance supervision;
- pension savings supervision;
- financial mediation and financial advisory supervision;
- foreign exchange supervision.

Banking Industry Supervision

[107] In the context of M&A activity relating to the banking industry, prior approval of the National Bank of Slovakia is required to acquire a qualified shareholding in a bank or exceed qualified interest in a bank so that the interest in share capital of the bank or voting rights of the bank reaches or exceeds 20%, 30% or 50% or so that the bank becomes a subsidiary of a person which acquires such interest in one or several operations directly or by action in concert.

[108] A person intending to cancel a qualified shareholding in a bank or to reduce his or her share in the share capital or voting rights of a bank below 20%, 30% or 50%, or so that the bank ceases to be its subsidiary company, must notify the National Bank of Slovakia thereof in advance in writing.

[109] The Securities Act defines the 'qualified shareholding' as a direct or indirect share in a legal entity, representing 10% or more of its share capital or voting rights or a share allowing exercise of significant influence over the management of that legal entity.

[110] In practice, the National Bank of Slovakia is typically approachable and cooperative in respect of various queries regarding the banking sector supervision (including the M&A transactions regarding the financial institutions). The formal proceedings before the National Bank of Slovakia are governed by special laws which are generally not onerous.

[111] The National Bank of Slovakia enjoys a relatively long statutory periods for granting approvals; generally the National Bank of Slovakia has three month period to grant approval/consent with the acquisition of shareholding in regulated entities. In respect of granting licences, the period is longer and is generally six months; however in practice, the National Bank of Slovakia tends to issue approvals/consents before the expiry of the statutory periods.

Securities Market Supervision

[112] The National Bank of Slovakia further performs securities market supervision, namely supervision over stock exchange, central depository of securities and certain other financial institutions such as investment guarantee fund, collective investment, investment firms.

[113] In respect of the public M&A transactions, the National Bank of Slovakia oversees the takeover bids, squeeze-outs/sell-outs as well as public offers of securities.

[114] Similarly, to the banking industry, in general, a prior approval of the National Bank of Slovakia is required to acquire a qualified shareholding (as defined below) in or exceed qualified interest in regulated entities. In addition the prior approval is required in case the aforementioned entities become a subsidiary of a person which acquires such interest in one or several operations directly or by action in concert.

[115] Furthermore, generally a person intending to cancel a qualified shareholding in the regulated entities or to reduce its share in the share capital or voting rights of such entities below certain percentage, or so that the such entity ceases to be its subsidiary company, must notify the National Bank of Slovakia thereof in advance in writing.

[116] In addition, in the M&A context, below we briefly set out the scene of the functioning of the stock exchange in Slovakia including the general overview of the trading with securities and insider trading legislation. In addition, the role of the central depository of securities is described.

Stock Exchange

General

[117] The operation of the stock exchange is subject to a licence issued by the National Bank of Slovakia. The stock exchange is based on a membership principle, meaning that only members that are investment firms, management companies, foreign investment firms, or alternatively foreign management companies may become a stock exchange members and conclude stock exchange transactions.

[118] Bratislava Stock Exchange is the sole operator of a regulated market of securities in Slovakia as well as the operator of a Multilateral Trading Facility. Bratislava Stock Exchange is a full member of the Federation of European Securities Exchanges.

[119] In practice, due to undeveloped capital markets in Slovakia, the trading on the stock exchange is virtually non-existent. In addition, there are few quoted companies on the Bratislava Stock Exchange; with the trend being that the companies are de-listing from the Bratislava Stock Exchange.

General Overview of the Trading with Securities

[120] Securities may be traded on public markets if admitted to trading on a regulated market or a Multilateral Trading Facility.

[121] Currently, the regulated markets in Slovakia are the following: (i) listed securities market, composed of (a) listed primary market, (b) listed parallel market, and (c) listed new market; and (ii) regulated free market. The operator is the Bratislava Stock Exchange.

[122] A security may be admitted to the relevant stock exchange market only if this security and its issuer meet the conditions under the Stock Exchange Act, a special regulation and the stock exchange rules.

[123] The admission of a security to a listed securities market must be requested by the security's issuer or by a stock exchange member through its issuer.

[124] A security may be admitted to the relevant stock exchange market only if it and its issuer meet the conditions under the Stock Exchange Act. For example, these include the following:

- a security is a financial instrument, as defined by the Securities Act;
- it is a fungible/interchangeable security;
- its transferability is not limited;
- it is a de-materialized (book-entered) security;
- in general, prospectus has been approved and published.

[125] Trading in the security on a stock exchange market may commence at the earliest on the day following the prospectus publication date.

[126] Placement of securities on a listed primary market and parallel market results in information duties for the issuer to its investors and the stock exchange, as detailed in the Rules for Acceptance of Securities to Bratislava Stock Exchange listed primary market and Rules for Acceptance of Securities to Bratislava Stock Exchange listed parallel market.

[127] Where a shareholder acquires or disposes of shares of an issuer whose shares are admitted to trading on a Regulated Market and to which voting rights are attached, such shareholder is under an obligation to notify the issuer of the proportion of voting rights of the issuer held by the shareholder as a result of the acquisition or disposal where that proportion reaches, exceeds or falls below the thresholds of 5%, 10%, 15%, 20%, 25%, 30%, 50% and 75%.

Insider Information/Insider Dealings

[128] The Securities Act also lays down a special regime for the protection of 'insider information'. The Slovak law defines insider information as information of a precise nature that has not been made public and that relates, directly or indirectly, to one or more issuers of financial instruments or to one or more financial instruments and which, if it were made public, would be likely to have a significant effect on the prices of those financial instruments or on the price of related derivative financial instruments.

[129] For persons charged with the execution of orders concerning financial instruments, insider information means information conveyed by a client and related to the client's pending orders, that is of a precise nature and which relates directly or indirectly to one or more issuers of financial instruments or to one or more financial instruments, and which, if it were made public, would be likely to have a significant effect on the price of those financial instruments or on the price of related derivative financial instruments.

[130] Should insider information be disclosed in the process of a due diligence review, such insider information must be made public by the issuer without delay. The issuer is not required to make public disclosure of the insider information if the person to whom the information was made available owes a confidentiality obligation under specific laws, articles of association or a contract.

[131] An issuer must also (i) maintain a list of entities who can access its insider information, and (ii) provide this list to the National Bank of Slovakia on its request without delay.

Central Depository of Securities

[132] The operation of the central cepository of Securities of the Slovak Republic (the 'CSD') is subject to a licence issued by the National Bank of Slovakia. At present, two entities in Slovakia have such licence to operate the CSD: (i) Centrálny depozitár cenných papierov SR, a.s. and (ii) Národný centrálny depozitár cenných papierov, a. s. The main duties of the CSD in the M&A context include registration of book-entry securities and provision of services related to recording process over securities.

[133] In practice, the CSD (especially Centrálny depozitár cenných papierov SR, a.s.) has a reputation of being a bureaucratic institution which is routinely known to impede transactions (both in terms of (i) M&A transactions in case of transfer of book-entered shares and (ii) bank financings put in place in connection with the M&A and namely concerning the registration of a security over shares).

[134] The registration process before CSD is governed by rules of operation which consist of a rather onerous set of rules which on instances are even contradictory to the existing law. In addition to the rules of operation, the CSD routinely requests additional documentation and evidence to be supplied during the registrations. Irrespective, the rules of operation and requests of CSD must be observed for CSD to perform the registrations.

[135] In terms of timing, the registration process should take up to fifteen days. However in practice, on occasions, the registration process may run into months, especially in case the CSD requests that additional documents are produced.

Competition Authorities

[136] In the context of M&A activity, the Antimonopoly Office clears mergers that meet the notification criteria.

[137] The notification criteria and the role of the Antimonopoly Office including the clearance process is further described in **paragraph [349]–[386]** (Merger Control).

Energy Regulatory Authorities

[138] The Regulatory Office for Network Industries is the regulatory and supervision authority over all types of network industries – electricity, gas, heat and water management industries.

[139] The Regulatory Office oversees activities such as the (i) generation, transmission, distribution and supply of electricity and the related services, (ii) performance of the short-term electricity market administrator's activities, (iii) production, transport, distribution, storage and supply of gas and the related services, (iv) production, distribution and supply of heat, (v) production, distribution and supply of water by public water supply system, (vi) diversion and purification of sewage through public sewerage system, (vii) abstraction of surface water and energy water from water flows, utilization of the hydro-potential of the water flows.

[140] However, the M&A transactions (both private and public) in the aforementioned network industries are not subject to consents/approvals by the Regulatory Office for Network Industries. Nevertheless, such M&A transactions must observe the applicable unbundling rules (which are generally based on the EU legislation) otherwise the Regulatory Office for Network Industries will impose corrective measures including the fines.

Company/Corporation Authorities

[141] There are no general company/corporation regulatory authorities in Slovakia which consent would be required for the purpose of M&A transactions.

[142] Irrespective, private M&A transactions are significantly affected by the registration of the transfer of the shares (ownership interest) in the limited liability company in the Commercial Register. Namely the transfer of the majority of shares (>50%) in the limited liability company is only effective once registered with the Commercial Register. Such registration will only be performed by the Commercial Register upon the tax authority confirmation that there are no outstanding tax liabilities pertaining the target company or the parties to the Sales and Purchase Agreement (SPA) if the transferor or transferee is listed on the list of tax debtors.

[143] The transfer of shares in the joint stock company or simplified joint stock company is not affected by the registration in the Commercial Register; securities in certificated form require physical delivery and endorsement by the transferor. Book-entered securities require registration of the transfer in the CSD.

CONTROLS/RESTRICTIONS ON FOREIGN INVESTMENT

General

[144] Slovak law provides for equal rights and obligations of both Slovak and foreign investors/investments. Accordingly, no foreign ownership restrictions apply save for certain narrow exceptions as described below. In addition, no local partner is required for a foreign-owned company to conduct its business or to trade in Slovakia.

[145] Slovakia does not impose any minimum or maximum foreign ownership restrictions. A foreign purchaser may freely acquire a 100% interest in Slovak entities. Furthermore, no formal approvals of the regulatory/governmental authorities are required that would go over and above the approvals required for domestic legal entities.

[146] Slovakia further does not impose restrictions on foreign investments in specifically regulated areas (such as defence, banking, utilities, energy markets etc.).

[147] In addition, the law does not impose any specific restrictions on foreign directors or managers. In principle, foreign directors or managers which are also members of statutory bodies (same as the Slovak directors/managers) must have a clean criminal record.

[148] In certain circumstances, however, foreign legal entities are subject to laws and regulations over and above those imposed on Slovak legal entities; such controls relate to the exchange control rules and acquisition of real estate by foreigners.

Exchange Control

[149] The Foreign Exchange Act does not, in principle, limit payments of capital to and from Slovakia. In general, there are no restrictions on Slovak legal entities or individuals having their bank accounts abroad.

[150] National Bank of Slovakia may impose a depositary duty in accordance with the Foreign Exchange Act. The depositary duty is an obligation on the part of legal entities and individuals to keep a specified percentage of funds for a certain period of time on a special account at the bank in the interests of currency stability.

[151] As long as the depositary duty persists, the legal entities and individuals that are under such obligation may not freely use the funds on this account and may not transfer their rights to use such funds to other persons.

[152] Under the Foreign Exchange Act, the Slovak government may declare a state of emergency in foreign exchange management for a maximum of three months if there is a direct and serious threat to the solvency of Slovakia. In this case, it is prohibited to (i) acquire foreign exchange assets in return for Euros by residents and non-residents, (ii) make any payments from Slovakia to a foreign country, including transfers of funds between banks and their branches; and (iii) deposit funds in accounts abroad.

[153] Further, if there is a serious threat to internal monetary balance of Slovakia, it is prohibited to (i) sell domestic securities to non-residents, (ii) accept financial credits from non-residents, (iii) open accounts in the country by non-residents and the deposit of funds in the accounts of non-residents, and (iv) transfer funds from abroad between banks and their branches.

[154] However, the above restrictions may only be imposed in exceptional situations; no such restrictions have been imposed to date, and none are expected in the near future.

Acquisition of Real Estate by Non-Residents

[155] Before joining the EU, the Slovak Republic agreed to gradually relax its restrictions on the acquisition of real estate by non-residents.

[156] The Foreign Exchange Act still restricts the acquisition of real estate by non-residents in certain ways. The general prohibition on the acquisition of agricultural and forest land has been lifted to date. However, non-residents can only acquire ownership of real property which acquisition is not prohibited or otherwise limited by various special laws. Such special laws include:

- Act No. 543/2002 Coll., on Nature and Landscape Protection, as amended.
- Act No. 326/2005 Coll., on Forests, as amended.
- Act No. 140/2014 Coll., on Acquisition of Ownership to Agricultural Lands.

[157] For illustration, under the Act on Acquisition of Ownership to Agricultural Lands, acquiring ownership of agricultural land is not allowed by (i) citizens of states, (ii) companies resident in states or (iii) states and their administrative units, which legal system does not allow Slovak citizens or legal entities to acquire agricultural lands in such state. This reciprocity restriction does not generally apply to EU Member States, the European Economic Area (EEA) and to natural persons with residence or legal persons with registered seat in such states.

Foreign Directors

[158] Local directors are not required to be members of the board or to be otherwise present in other elements of the corporate structure (such as supervisory body). Neither the presence of any governmental/state official required on a supervisory basis (although in companies with state/government stake this tends to be the case).

[159] In essence, the shareholders of a Slovak company are free to choose its directors, such directors can only be natural persons (the Slovak law to date does not allow a legal entity to be a director). Directors may sit outside Slovakia, with the day-to-day business being conducted by managers under the power of attorney granted by the directors.

[160] Otherwise, a foreign individual performing duties as a member of an executive body of a Slovak company while residing in Slovakia must apply for a visa for a stay in Slovakia unless he or she is a citizen of the EU or unless a specific exemption applies to such person's country of origin.

[161] Visa for a stay not exceeding three months is issued after all the statutory requirements (such as possession of sufficient funds, housing in Slovakia and a clean criminal record) have been satisfied and proven. Visa may be extended repeatedly. Should the stay exceed three months, the foreign citizen must apply for a temporary or permanent residence in Slovakia under the conditions set out by the Foreign Nationals Residence Act.

[162] Extract from the Criminal Register, or an equivalent document from the country of origin or a country in which the foreign citizen has stayed for six consecutive months in the last five years, must be submitted to the trade office maintaining the small trade registry.

[163] The above rules (except for the obligation to present the Criminal Register extract) do not apply to citizens of the EU, who can stay and perform duties of a member of an executive body of a Slovak company in Slovakia without restrictions.

INCENTIVES FOR FOREIGN INVESTMENT

General

[164] Investors who locate their investments in Slovakia can obtain aid in the form of investment incentives. Granting of investment incentives is no longer as popular and as frequent as it used to be in the previous decade, however, there is still a realistic chance that new projects or significant expansions of existing projects by investors in Slovakia would receive aid in one of the forms described below.

[165] Only a legal entity with its registered office in Slovakia can be a recipient of investment incentives. Investment incentives are granted under the Act No. 57/2018 on Regional Investment Aid and can take one of the following forms:

(i) corporate tax relief;
(ii) job creation grants;
(iii) capital investment grants (now quite rare and being phased-out by the government); and
(iv) site support (acquisition or lease of land below market value).

[166] Three categories of projects (industries) are supported under the Regional Investment Aid Act:

(i) manufacturing industry;
(ii) technological (R&D) centres; and
(iii) shared service centres (or combination of technological and shared service centres).

[167] Regional Investment Aid Act details, for each type of project, conditions which must be fulfilled in order for the investor to apply for investment incentives, such as e.g. minimum capital investment, minimum number of jobs created, education levels of employees in technological and service centres etc.). The approval process can be rather burdensome and may take twelve months or even more, depending on circumstances. There is no automatic right of an investor to receive incentives if the investor meets conditions prescribed by law – decision to grant incentives is discretionary by the government.

[168] For each project, the conditions must be fulfilled within three years (five years for large projects) of the date on which the investment incentives are granted (i.e. the issuance of the decision to grant investment incentives). The recipient must not start work on the project (i.e. shall not acquire any assets – including orders of machines and equipment – and shall not commence construction works or hiring of employees) prior to the issuance of the confirmation of registration of the project by the government (incentive effect of the aid must be demonstrated), and that the recipient shall retain the required assets and created jobs throughout the entire period of its utilising state aid (at least for a period of five years).

[169] In order to receive state aid, the investor must fully disclose its ownership structure up to ultimate beneficial owners. Ownership structure must be disclosed in a public online register called a 'Register of Public Sector Partners'.

The Regional Investment Aid Act has been approved by the European Commission as an aid scheme compatible with the common market and, as such, incentives granted by Slovak government under the Investment Aid Act do not require any further clearances at the EU level.

Tax Relief

[170] The tax incentive has two forms. If a new company is established for the investment project, the new company is eligible for corporate income tax relief for up to ten years. If the investment takes the form of an expansion project within an existing company, such company is eligible for pro-rated corporate income tax relief for up to ten years. The tax relief is terminated when the company has reached the maximum allowed state aid intensity, which varies by regions.

Job-Creation Grants

[171] Job-creation grants of up to 60% of eligible wage costs can be provided by local labour offices, depending on levels of unemployment in the region where the new jobs are created.

Cash Grant on Capital Investment

[172] Cash grant on capital investment is available only to strategic investment projects and is seen less often than in the past. No grants are provided in the Bratislava region. This support is available for projects in manufacturing industry and technological centres. Decisions concerning support to eligible projects will be made by the government.

Site Support

[173] The preferential transfer of land or land with infrastructure owned by the state or municipalities is possible, depending on the landowner's agreement to such preferential transfer.

SARIO[3]

[174] The main state agency dealing with incentives for foreign investment is the Slovak Investment and Trade Development Agency (SARIO in Slovak). It is an agency founded and run by the Ministry of Industry. SARIO contributes to attracting foreign investment and developing domestic companies through its services and development programmes.

[175] SARIO is exclusively authorized to file applications for investment incentives with the competent governing bodies and prepares draft offers to grant investment incentives for investors. Its task is also to provide potential investors current data and information on business climate, investment environment and investment opportunities in Slovakia.

SPECIFIC ISSUES OF COMPANY/SECURITIES LAW

[176] The Slovak legal framework regarding company/securities law remains largely influenced by the EU law, especially in respect of the securities where the legislation draws heavily on the EU securities directives and regulations.

Shareholder Approval

[177] Under the law shareholders' approval rights in respect of M&A transactions vary depending on the type of the target company – whether it is a limited liability company or a joint stock company. Shareholder approval of the target company is required in particular, for:

(a) sale of shareholding interest in a limited liability company to an existing shareholder of the target company unless stipulated otherwise in the target company's constitutional documents;
(b) sale of shareholding interest in a limited liability company to a third party if required under the target's constitutional documents;
(c) sale of shares in a joint stock company to the extent required under the target's constitutional documents;
(d) sale of enterprise or a part thereof;
(e) merger of the target company.

[178] Shareholder approval takes a form of a resolution of the general meeting of the target company or a resolution of the target company's sole shareholder. Shareholder approval for the seller and the purchaser is not prescribed by Slovak law. In case the sellers/purchasers are foreign entities, such shareholder approval may be

[3] http://www.sario.sk/en.

required by the law of incorporation of the relevant seller/purchaser. Notwithstanding the above, shareholder approval for the seller and purchaser may be required under the seller's/purchaser's constitutional documents.

[179] Simple majority of votes is normally sufficient to achieve shareholder approval of M&A transactions; the constitutional documents of the target may require higher thresholds.

Directors' Duties

[180] The directors are under a duty to exercise their powers with due professional care in the best interests of the company and all its shareholders. This means the interests of the company itself and not the group of which it is a member.

[181] The director cannot prefer its own interest, interests of some shareholders or third persons over the company's interests. Directors that infringe their obligations are jointly and severally responsible to the company for any damage caused. The director shall not be liable for damage if he proves that during the performance of his functions has proceeded with due care and in good faith, and that he was acting in the interests of the company. Executives are not be liable for damages caused to the company through actions where they executed a resolution of the company's general meeting. However, this exemption shall not apply such resolution is contrary to applicable laws or the constitutional documents of the company.

[182] As a general rule, no person may give instructions to the directors concerning the management of a company's business – the directors are required to exercise their own judgment.

[183] Agreements between the company and the directors excluding or limiting the liability of the directors towards the company are forbidden. Neither the Memorandum of Association nor the Articles of Association may limit or exclude the liability of the director.

[184] The company may waive its claims to damages against executives or agree upon a settlement with them not sooner than three years after the occurrence of the relevant events, provided that the General Meeting approves it and provided that shareholder(s) holding 5% (10% in the case of a limited liability company) of the registered capital do not raise an objection against such decision.

[185] In some circumstances, a creditor of the company may lodge a claim for damages against a director of a company in his own name and on his own account in respect of damages suffered by the creditor vis-à-vis the company, if he cannot satisfy his claim from assets of the company. Claims of the creditors of the company against the directors are not extinguished if the company waives claims to damages or concludes an agreement on settlement with the creditors. If a bankruptcy proceeding is initiated in respect of the company, the bankruptcy trustee will lodge claims of the creditors of the company against the directors.

[186] In order to minimize the risk of breaching director's duties, the general meeting of the company would approve documents signed by the company in the transaction and explicitly authorize directors to sign any and all documentation relating to the transaction.

Form of Consideration

[187] Consideration may be paid up in money or in securities or as a combination of both. If part of the consideration is offered as securities, the offeror must also offer, as an alternative, corresponding consideration in money.

[188] Shares can be issued for a non-cash consideration – in kind contributions, such as the contribution of assets. Under the law only assets/property which economic value can be determined may be a considered as an in kind contribution.

[189] However contribution of services is not allowed. Contributions consisting of a commitment to carry out certain works or to provide certain services are not allowed.

Financial Assistance

[190] A Slovak joint stock company may not grant advance payments nor loans in relation to the acquisition of its (or its parent's) shares and it may not secure any loans for such purposes nor any other liabilities relating to the acquisition of its shares.

[191] The financial assistance prohibition does not apply to a limited liability company. However, if the parent of the limited liability company is a joint stock company, it may not grant to the limited liability subsidiary advance payments or any loans for the purpose of acquiring shares of the parent company, which is a joint stock company.

[192] Under certain conditions, the prohibition does not apply to (a) transactions involving the acquisition of shares by or for employees of the company and (b) banks (if carrying out their common banking activities).

[193] In an acquisition financing, the Slovak target and its Slovak subsidiaries (controlled companies) will generally not be able to provide security in relation to the acquisition facility. This will, according to the prevailing view, extend to any acquisition refinancing. Non-Slovak subsidiaries of a Slovak target are not caught by this prohibition but are subject to any financial assistance restrictions in the jurisdiction of such subsidiary.

[194] Shares in the Slovak target held by the acquirer prior to the transaction may be used for securing the acquisition facility without breaching the financial assistance prohibition.

[195] Distribution of dividends by the Slovak target to the acquirer or a capital decrease of the Slovak target resulting in an equity distribution which will be used to repay a loan incurred in connection with the acquisition of the Slovak target's shares is permitted.

[196] Another widely used method is an upstream merger of the Slovak bid company and the Slovak target. The Slovak target will merge into the Slovak bid company and, after the merger, the Slovak bid company may secure the acquisition or refinancing loan by assets formerly owned by the Slovak target.

[197] Provision by a Slovak joint stock company of a loan or a borrowing, transfer or making available for use the property of the Slovak company or securing a liability of specified persons (such as director, proxy (*prokurista*) or other person authorized to act for the company, or persons close to them or persons who act on their account) can be concluded only:

(i) after previous approval of a supervisory board; and
(ii) under arm's length terms.

[198] The approval by the supervisory board is not required if a controlling entity is to provide a loan or a borrowing, transfer or make available for use its property or securing a liability of a controlled entity (downstream guarantee or security).

[199] There is no whitewash procedure applicable under Slovak law.

Security Interests

[200] There are several types of assets suitable for security under Slovak law, specified below.

[201] There is no exact equivalent concept of a floating charge in Slovak law. The closest form is probably the combination of the pledge of an enterprise or of a part of an enterprise (if there is any) with pledge over any assets which the pledgor will acquire in the future. Both of these forms of pledges must be registered with the Notarial Central Register of Pledges ('**Register**') and, if required by special law, also in special register(s) (i.e. Real Estate Register, register of pledges over ships, planes etc.).

[202] A company may have one or more enterprises (economic and accounting unit(s)). Each enterprise may be the subject of transfer separately from the other assets and liabilities of the company (or other enterprise(s), if any). It is not recommended to rely solely on the pledge of an enterprise as the only security securing a particular claim. The reason is that even if an enterprise is pledged, the individual assets forming the pledged enterprise will not be subject to the pledge when the asset is sold. This means that if the debtor disposes of them, the secured creditor would have no proprietary right against the individual persons that acquired the assets.

[203] If a pledge over the assets which the pledgor acquires in the future is registered with the Register, the pledge over any new asset becomes valid and effective as of the day of acquisition of ownership of the asset(s) by the pledgor. If the asset requires further registration in a special register(s), such register is obliged to register creation of the pledge over the asset as of the day of acquisition of ownership of the asset by the pledgor.

[204] As a general rule, security has an accessory nature and there is no security without a secured receivable. There are some exceptions to this rule (for example, bank guarantees). Pledges can secure financial or non-financial receivable(s), future receivable(s) or conditional receivable(s). Virtually any transferable asset, right, collection of things and/or other kind of tangible value can be subject of a pledge as a collateral, with certain specific exceptions set out in the Slovak laws.

[205] A pledge follows the collateral and the receivable to which it is attached (i.e. if the receivable that is secured by a pledge over the pledgor's asset is assigned to third person, the third person becomes the new pledgee with all rights and obligations of the original pledgee with respect to the pledged collateral).

[206] Any agreement prohibiting the creation of a pledge is unenforceable towards third persons.

[207] The pledge can be enforced by the pledgee if the secured receivable or any of its part is not paid when due and payable. If agreed under the pledge agreement the pledgee is entitled to sell the collateral or run a public tender or sell the collateral at a voluntary auction. When selling the collateral the pledgee acts in the name of the pledgor.

Pledge of Shares

[208] Shareholders of a joint-stock company often secure loans granted to the joint-stock company (particularly if the joint-stock company is a controlled entity) by pledging their shares in the joint-stock company to the lender (a bank).

[209] The pledge of share certificates is created under a written pledge agreement, written confirmation on the content of the pledge agreement (pledgor's signature shall be certified by a notary public), endorsement of the pledge on the backside of share certificates, their handing-over to the pledgee and is perfected by registration with the CSD. The endorsement must contain the note 'subject to lien' and must identify the pledgee.

[210] In the case of de-materialized (book-entered) shares, the pledge is effected by execution of a written pledge agreement, written confirmation on the content of the pledge agreement (pledgor's signature must be certified by a notary public) and is perfected by registration with the CSD.

[211] Pledged shares cannot be further pledged. The pledge also applies to yields on the pledged shares.

[212] If the articles of association require the transfer of registered shares to be approved by the company (or if there is another condition precedent which needs to be fulfilled), the pledge must also be so approved (or the condition precedent must be fulfilled).

[213] If the debt secured by pledged shares is not settled fully and on time, the pledgee is entitled to sell the shares through a brokerage firm. The pledgee must inform the pledgor of the intended sale before it takes place unless the relevant pledge agreement provides otherwise.

Pledge of Ownership Interest in a Limited Liability Company

[214] A written agreement with notarized signatures of both parties is required for creation of pledge over ownership interest in a limited liability company. If the memorandum of association requires the general meeting's consent to the ownership interest transfer or if there is some other condition precedent that needs to be fulfilled, such consent is also required (or the condition precedent must be fulfilled) before the ownership interest is pledged, otherwise the pledge will not be created. The pledge becomes perfected upon its registration in the Commercial Register.

[215] While an ownership interest is pledged, the shareholder exercises the rights that are attached to that ownership interest in the limited liability company. A pledged ownership interest may be re-pledged.

[216] If the debt secured by pledged ownership interest is not settled fully and on time, the pledgee can enforce the pledge by selling the ownership interest at a public auction or by other means agreed in the pledge agreement (usually by direct sale or in a public tender).

Pledge of Movables and Receivables

[217] Pledge of movable assets is created upon written pledge agreement and is perfected upon registration in the Register. Alternatively, the pledge can be perfected upon the handing-over of the assets by the pledgee without the need to sign the pledge agreement or register the pledge. Such pledge can be anytime registered in the Register afterwards, however if the pledge was not created under the written pledge agreement, the pledgee and the pledgor are obliged to sign the written confirmation on the content of the pledge agreement before the pledge is registered in the Register.

[218] Pledge of receivables is created upon written pledge agreement and is perfected upon registration in the Register. To take effect against the debtor, notification of the pledge to the sub-debtor is required. Only freely transferable receivables may be pledged.

Mortgages

[219] A mortgage over real property can be created under a written contract between the owner of the property and the creditor of the secured receivable. A mortgage agreement must contain detailed identification of the property over which the mortgage is being established and the identification of the secured receivable. A foreign lender may take security over local immovable property.

[220] To become perfected, the mortgage over real property registered with the Real Estate Register must also be registered in the Real Estate Register by a specific application.

Completion Formalities

Real Estate

[221] A written agreement with a notarized signature of the transferor(s) and the registration of the transfer of an ownership right in the Real Estate Register is required for transfer of real estate. Depending on the place of signing the signature of the transferor may need to be also apostilled or superlegalized.

[222] The transfer takes effect as of its registration in the Real Estate Register. It is necessary to include the signatures on the same document/instrument – i.e. in respect of M&A real estate transactions (such as asset deals) it is not possible to sign the transfer agreement in counterparts.

[223] The registration takes up to thirty days, however, it is possible to pay for the expedited registration which takes up to fifteen days. In practice, the expedited registration is commonly used.

Transfer of Ownership Interest in Limited Liability Company

[224] A written agreement with notarized signatures of all parties thereto is required for a transfer of an ownership interest in a limited liability company. The transfer needs to be registered in the Commercial Register.

[225] Registration in the Commercial Register is of a declaratory nature, save for the transfer of a majority ownership interest in which case its transfer takes effect only as of its registration in the Commercial Register.

[226] An ownership interest to which at least half of the voting rights are attached is considered a majority shareholding interest.

[227] Prior the transfer of majority ownership interest – both the transferee and the transferor must evidence to the Commercial Register a consent of the tax authority certifying that no tax liabilities are outstanding by both of them.

Transfer of Shares in a Joint Stock Company

[228] The shares in a joint stock company can have the form of certificated registered shares (physical shares) and book-entered shares. In practice, the common form of shares used by the companies are the certificated registered shares. Book-entered shares are typical in respect financial institutions, such as banks.

Certificated Registered Shares

[229] An endorsement and hand-over is required for a transfer of certificated registered shares. The transfer itself is completed upon the endorsement and hand-over of shares and is not required to be registered in the Commercial Register, however a change in the shareholder's structure (which is a logical result of the transfer) requires to be registered, provided that the company has a sole shareholder.

Book-Entered Shares

[230] An agreement and registration of the book-entered shares on the owner's account maintained by CSD is required for a transfer of book-entered shares. The transfer itself is not required to be registered in the Commercial Register, it is completed upon the registration with the CSD. However, a change in the shareholder's structure (which is a logical result of the transfer) requires to be registered in the Commercial Register, provided that the company has a sole shareholder.

Enterprise

[231] An agreement with notarized signatures of the seller(s) and the purchaser(s) and registration of the transfer in the Commercial Register is required for a transfer of an enterprise.

Movable Property

[232] Transfers of movable property, such as machinery, vehicles and physical stock, require actual handover in addition to a legally binding transfer agreement in order for the title to pass to the purchaser. The transfer agreement as such does not need to be in writing, but written form is recommended.

Receivables

[233] Receivables are transferred by an assignment agreement, which must be in writing. Unless agreed otherwise, the debtor's consent to the assignment is not required. Once the assignment is notified to the debtor by the assignor or proven by the assignee, the debtor is able to discharge itself of its obligation only by performing its obligations to the assignee and not to the assignor.

[234] However, the whole contract (akin to English novation) as such cannot be assigned under Slovak law. The common approach is to enter into an agreement containing agreement of the parties on the assignment of receivables and an agreement on assumption of debts.

Intellectual Property Rights

[235] The transfer of intellectual property rights may require registration in a public register (for example, trademarks and patents). A company's business name registered in the Commercial Register may not be transferred without the simultaneous transfer of the business to which it relates.

Licences

[236] Licences granted under public law may not generally be transferred. Even if a licence has been issued for the operation of an appliance, the new operator will usually need to apply for a new licence from the relevant authority.

Employees

[237] If a significant portion of assets relating to certain business activities that will be newly carried out by the transferee of the assets is transferred, employees attributable to such assets may pass by operation of law to the transferee.

Costs and Fees

[238] Certain M&A transactions are subject to registration(s) in public registries and/or require notarization of signatures on the transfer agreement.

[239] Fees to be paid in connection with such registrations and notarizations are rather low, save for registration of a transfer of a large number of shares with the CSD or execution of a notarial deed as an execution title for a large amount in connection with an M&A transaction.

Dividends

[240] Shareholders participate in the profits of a Slovak joint-stock company or limited liability company through dividends approved by the general meeting of shareholders. Dividends may only be paid when the general meeting has approved the payment of dividends on the basis of the company's economic performance, as set out in the annual statement.

[241] The company must not pay any interest on contributions made to the company and advances for the account of dividends. The shareholders may not require a redemption of their contributions for the entire term of existence of the company. The shareholders shall be obliged to refund to the company any profits paid to them in breach of the above. The executive directors who have approved such payments shall bear joint and several liability for the refund above.

[242] The company is allowed to distribute among the shareholders only the net profits which must be (i) reduced by the amount appropriated to the reserve fund or other funds, as appropriate which the company has established under the law, and reduced by any loss brought forward and (ii) increased by the profits brought forward (retained earnings) and the funds established out of profits, the use of which is not prescribed by the law.

[243] Further, the right to receive dividends can only be transferred separately after the decision of the general meeting on dividends has been taken.

[244] The target company in an M&A deal cannot distribute the profits gained in the same financial year among the selling shareholders and therefore the common approach is to increase the purchase price by the amount of such profits.

Purchase of Own Shares

[245] As a general rule, a limited liability company and a joint stock company cannot acquire its own shares (shareholding interests). There are some exemptions to this rule, set out below.

[246] If a limited liability company acquires its own ownership interests (or if a controlled entity acquires shareholding interest of a controlling entity) in accordance with the laws (e.g. as a consequence of dismissal of a shareholder), it shall not be allowed to exercise the rights of a shareholder and the company shall (i) transfer such shareholding interest to an another shareholder or third party, or if not transferred within six months (ii) decrease the registered capital by the amount of a contribution attributable to such shareholding interest, otherwise a competent court may decide on dissolution of such company.

[247] If shares of a joint stock company are subscribed by a party acting in its own name, but for the account of the company, the shares shall be deemed to be subscribed for its own account and the party shall be obliged to pay up the issue price of such shares. Furthermore, a joint stock company may acquire its own shares in cases specified in the Commercial Code. In all cases the company is obliged to transfer such shares in one year (in certain cases three years) or decrease the registered capital, otherwise a competent court may decide on dissolution of such company. No shareholder rights can be exercised by the company in relation to these shares.

The Corporate Veil

[248] The Slovak law does not expressly recognize piercing of the corporate veil nor have the courts developed such a concept. Accordingly, the parent company (shareholder) cannot be held liable for the debts or liabilities of its Slovak subsidiary – either a limited company or the joint stock company.

[249] Certain arguments have been made in support of piercing the corporate veil – however, in the absence of a court decisions such arguments remain largely theoretical. Accordingly, Slovak law seems to afford full protection to the corporate shield and the use of corporate structures to mitigate liability of shareholders.

[250] Irrespective of the above, the shareholder of a Slovak limited liability company guarantees the subsidiary's debts:

(a) to the extent of its outstanding contribution to the subsidiary's registered capital; consequently, such guarantee ceases to exist once the parent company's contribution to the subsidiary's registered capital is fully paid up and registered in the Commercial Register;
(b) in case of bankruptcy of the subsidiary, provided the creditors who have registered their claims in the bankruptcy have not been satisfied in full and to the extent, the parent's/shareholder's guarantee has not ceased to exist prior to the bankruptcy proceedings;
(c) even after dissolution of the subsidiary, to the extent of the received share on liquidation proceeds received by the parent/shareholder.

INSOLVENCY

[251] The main legal aspects of Slovak rules on insolvency are regulated by the Insolvency Code. In principle, the Insolvency Code recognizes three types of insolvency proceedings:

(i) bankruptcy;
(ii) restructuring; and
(iii) debt clearance.

[252] Besides these insolvency regimes, Slovak corporate law recognizes a voluntary winding-up of a company (liquidation), a feasible option for solvent companies.

[253] In addition, so-called company in crisis regime under the Commercial Code has been introduced several restrictions on acting of companies and their shareholders, if the financial position of the company deteriorates.

Bankruptcy

[254] There are two insolvency tests under Slovak legislation: a financial liquidity test and a test of over-indebtedness. If a company is illiquid and/or over-indebted, it is deemed insolvent under the Slovak law.

[255] A company is deemed illiquid if it is not able to pay its debts (two or more financial obligations) as they fall due for more than thirty days and has more than one creditor. An individual is deemed illiquid if he/she is not able to pay his/her debt as it falls due more than 180 days.

[256] A company is over-indebted if (a) it is obliged to keep accounting books under Slovak law (b) its liabilities exceed its total assets and (c) has more than one creditor. As a consequence, all liabilities of the company (not just overdue liabilities) shall be taken into account when assessing the financial condition of a company. Liabilities and assets are valued on the basis of (A) the company's books or (B) expert appraisal, which (if available) prevails over the data set out in the books, whereas the company's expected results (if further operation of the company is feasible) shall also be taken into account (i.e. going concern principle). Subordinated and similar claims shall not be included in assessment of a debtor's financial situation under the test of over-indebtedness.

[257] If a company is insolvent, bankruptcy may be declared on petition filed by the debtor or the creditor(s), however (i) creditors are only allowed to seek bankruptcy of a debtor based on a financial liquidity test, and (ii) debtors are only allowed to seek bankruptcy only in case of over indebtedness.

[258] A debtor and its directors have a duty to file a petition for bankruptcy within thirty days from the day on which they became aware of the company's over indebtedness or should have become aware if they had acted with due care. If the directors fail to file such a petition for bankruptcy within the deadline, they are (a) obliged to pay, as a contractual penalty established under the Insolvency Code, an amount equalling EUR12 500 and (b) liable for any loss suffered by the creditors of the insolvent debtor on top of such contractual penalty. The amount of loss is presumed as non-compensated amount of claims of the creditors in later insolvency proceedings.

[259] The Insolvency Code defines two main cornerstones of bankruptcy proceedings with far-reaching effects: (i) commencement of bankruptcy proceedings, and (ii) declaration of bankruptcy.

[260] Bankruptcy proceedings commence upon publication of a court decision on commencement of bankruptcy proceedings in the insolvency register. This means that:

(i) the debtor must restrict its business to ordinary course only;
(ii) no enforcement proceedings against assets owned by the debtor, other than the bankruptcy, is allowed and such proceedings that have been already opened are stayed;
(iii) no enforcement of pledge or mortgage against the debtor is permitted, save for certain statutory exceptions (such as cash collaterals, claims from bank accounts and certain transferable securities);
(iv) the proceedings on dissolution of the company (i.e. debtor) without legal successor are stayed; and
(v) merger, amalgamation or spin-off of the debtor is not permitted.

[261] Any acts by the debtor other than those performed in ordinary course of its business can be contested later in bankruptcy proceedings.

[262] A decision declaring the bankruptcy has the following effects:

(i) debtor's powers to manage and dispose with his or her property, and the power to act on behalf of the debtor, pass to the trustee;
(ii) any debtor's claims will be settled by trustee;
(iii) trustee is entitled to terminate debtor's contracts;
(iv) any debtor's receivables or payables not yet due accrued prior to the bankruptcy will be deemed due and payable;
(v) lawsuits and other proceedings will be stayed;
(vi) no enforcement actions are permitted against the assets comprising the bankruptcy estate;
(vii) no security may be established over any assets comprising the bankruptcy estate;
(viii) set-off of receivables against the debtor is restricted to a certain extent;
(ix) debtor's employment matters are managed by the trustee.

[263] In order to register creditor's claim in bankruptcy proceedings, the creditor must submit the claim to the trustee within a relatively short deadline – forty-five days from the declaration of bankruptcy, using an obligatory template application form. Any formal mistake or discrepancy when filing the data in the application form could render the application (and therefore the full claim) invalid, without any possibility for a creditor to correct it. The current legislation allows creditors to submit their claims even after the statutory period (forty-five days from the declaration of bankruptcy) has lapsed. However, those creditors will not have any voting rights in bankruptcy and, if the claim was secured, such security expires as of the date of expiration of the forty-five days period from the declaration of bankruptcy.

[264] The Insolvency Code also contains rules on when certain acts of the debtor could become ineffective ('contestable legal acts').

[265] No legal act performed by the debtor is ineffective as such; ineffectiveness must be claimed by the trustee or a creditor before the insolvency court. A petition for ineffectiveness may be filed within one year of declaration of bankruptcy. In accordance with the Insolvency Code, the debtor's legal acts may be proclaimed ineffective if they constitute:

(i) 'undervalues', that is, acts without adequate consideration;
(ii) 'preferences', that is, acts in preference of a certain creditor; or
(iii) 'fraudulent transfers', that is, acts intentionally preventing a creditor from being satisfied.

[266] There are certain time limits (one to five years prior to commencement of the bankruptcy proceedings) within which such contestable legal acts must have taken place. Applicable time limits vary depending on whether the person/entity benefiting from such act is related to the debtor. As a general rule, if a legal act is declared ineffective (contestable) by an insolvency court, the party that had benefit from the contestable legal act shall return to the debtor's insolvency estate any right or asset transferred from the debtor under such contestable legal act.

Restructuring

[267] Slovak companies in financial difficulties looking for a rescue solution may opt for either court (formal) restructuring or out-of-court (non-formal) restructuring process.

[268] Restructuring takes priority over bankruptcy. If a petition to initiate restructuring proceedings is submitted during the bankruptcy proceedings, the court would review this petition and, if it meets the prescribed requirements, the court would stay the bankruptcy proceedings and commence restructuring process. There is however important restrain on the court restructuring, which is the requirement that the compensation to general unsecured creditors in restructuring must be at least 50%, otherwise the court will not approve the final restructuring plan, except where concerned creditors expressly agree to a lower compensation. This recent rule has made the court restructuring significantly less prevalent in Slovakia.

[269] The debtor or (with the debtor's consent) any of its creditors may file for restructuring as a method to remedy insolvency. Restructuring is a court-driven rescue process available to businesses endangered by insolvency. It is aimed at proportional satisfaction of the creditors' claims through preparation and adoption of a restructuring plan and is designed to save the business (or at least its vital part) from liquidation. In the initial phase of restructuring, the debtor appoints a trustee to evaluate whether the business is suitable for restructuring (this stage takes about one month). Subject to receiving a positive trustee's opinion, restructuring proceedings co-managed by the debtor's management and the trustee (under the court and creditors supervision) follow. Restructuring proceedings take approximately six to eight months and the debtor enjoys a statutory protection from individual enforcement actions of creditors during this period. Restructuring takes priority over bankruptcy.

[270] Restructuring may be used only in these conditions:

- (i) the debtor is engaged in ongoing business;
- (ii) the debtor is endangered by or already suffers from insolvency;
- (iii) it is reasonable to expect that at least material part of the debtor's business will be maintained;
- (iv) if restructuring is permitted, it is reasonable to expect that the average satisfaction of the creditors will be higher compared to bankruptcy.

[271] The Insolvency Code defines two main cornerstones of the restructuring proceedings with far-reaching effects: (i) commencement of restructuring proceedings and the (ii) authorization of restructuring.

[272] The commencement of restructuring proceedings has the following effects:

- (i) the debtor must restrict its business to ordinary course only;
- (ii) creditors' claims and collaterals may not be enforced outside the restructuring;

(iii) third parties are not entitled to terminate any agreement with the debtor due to restructuring proceedings;
(iv) creditors' claims cannot be set off against those of the debtor.

[273] The effects of the decision of the insolvency court permitting the restructuring are in addition to the effects of the commencement of the restructuring proceedings described above and are as follows:

(i) in general, restructuring prevents the commencement or continuation of bankruptcy proceedings against the debtor;
(ii) any lawsuits or arbitrations concerning creditors' claims registered in restructuring are interrupted.

Sale of Shares or Business in Insolvency

[274] The shares or an enterprise of a Slovak entity being subject to bankruptcy proceedings under the law can only be sold by the bankruptcy trustee acting in the name and on behalf of the insolvent shareholder. Under certain conditions, the creditors' committee or another entitled party may give binding instructions to the bankruptcy trustee in connection with the realization of the assets of the insolvent entity.

[275] Shares or an enterprise are acquired from the bankruptcy trustee free of any encumbrances and there are no negative implications pertaining to the purchaser.

'Company in Crisis' Regime

[276] Recent amendments to the Commercial Code introduced several restrictions on acting of the company that is deemed to be 'in crisis'. A company is in crisis when it is insolvent (within the meaning of the Insolvency Act as described above) or at risk of becoming insolvent, which is the case if a company's equity-to-debt ratio is lower than 8/100.

[277] The directors of a company in crisis is under a general duty of care and must take all steps that would normally be taken by a reasonably diligent person to overcome the crisis.

[278] Generally, loans and similar payments extended to a company in crisis by its statutory body (director), a proxy, a member of the supervisory board, a shareholder holding at least 5% of capital, or an associated person (affiliate), are treated as equity under the special regime and any refund of such contributions by the company during the crisis is prohibited. Consequently, any such proceeds provided by the company in crisis must be returned back to the company. The statutory representatives of the company in crisis jointly and severally guarantee such obligation of the company in crisis.

[279] Further, when a security (guarantee, pledge, etc.) is provided by the above-mentioned persons to secure an obligation of a company in crisis, the company's creditor is entitled to be satisfied directly from such security, without the need to exercise its right against the company first (which would be the normal procedure). The above-mentioned persons may not be reimbursed for the provided security as long as the company remains in crisis or would become in crisis as a result.

[280] In addition, a lender providing loan to a Slovak company in crisis can be limited in satisfaction from the borrower's assets if there is a related party security granted and perfected at the time of crisis of the Slovak company and the lender has knowledge or potential knowledge about the crisis at the at the moment of signing and/or utilization. The affected lender can be satisfied from the borrower's assets only in an amount of difference between value of its receivables and the value of related party security.

CHOICE OF LAW

Governing Law

[281] The choice of a foreign law governing an agreement entered into by a Slovak entity will be valid under the conditions stipulated by Regulation (EC) No 593/2008 on the Law Applicable to Contractual Obligations (Rome I Regulation). In certain instances, the Rome Convention (1980 (Rome) Convention on the law applicable in contractual matters) or other applicable legal instrument may be relevant and applicable.

It is recommended that agreements relating to assets registered in public registers (real estate, shares in a limited liability company) or rights to be entered into public registers or a notarial register (e.g. pledge of receivables) be governed by Slovak law.

[282] With regards to the international sales law, there is the 1980 United Nations Convention on Contracts for the International Sale of Goods (CISG), an international treaty comprising the substantive law harmonization in the area of international sales. It has significant importance because it is widespread all over the world. Currently, ninety-one states ratified the CISG. In case the business parties to an international sales contract from the different Contracting States do not expressly exclude the application of the CISG, it will be directly applicable to their sales contract.

Jurisdiction

[283] Judgments obtained in other member countries of the EU (except for Denmark) are enforceable in Slovakia, in line with the Regulation (EC) No. 1215/2012 of 12 December 2012 on jurisdiction and the recognition and enforcement of judgments in civil and commercial matters (recast) (Brussels I bis Regulation). By a special agreement, the provisions of this legal instrument were extended also to Denmark.

[284] On the application of the interested party, a judgment of a foreign court of EU Member State shall not be recognized and enforced in Slovakia if:

(i) such recognition is manifestly contrary to public policy in the Slovak Republic;
(ii) the judgment was given in default of appearance, the defendant was not served with the document which instituted the proceedings or with an equivalent document in sufficient time and in such a way as to enable him to arrange for his defence, unless the defendant failed to commence proceedings to challenge the judgment when it was possible for him to do so;
(iii) the judgment is irreconcilable with a judgment given in a dispute between the same parties in the Slovak Republic;
(iv) the judgment is irreconcilable with an earlier judgment given in another EU Member State or in a third state involving the same cause of action and between the same parties, provided that the earlier judgment fulfils the conditions necessary for its recognition in the Slovak Republic;
(v) the judgment conflicts with the rules of the Brussels I bis Regulation governing jurisdiction in matters relating to insurance, jurisdiction over consumer contracts and exclusive jurisdiction.

[285] Under general statutory regulations, a decision of a foreign court (outside the EU Member States) shall not be recognized and enforced in Slovakia if:

(i) such foreign judgment relates to a matter which is within the exclusive competence of the authorities or courts of Slovak Republic;
(ii) according to Slovak law, the authorities or courts of that foreign state do not have competence to issue such judgment;
(iii) such foreign judgment is not final or enforceable in the state where it has been issued;
(iv) such foreign judgment is not a judgment on the merits of the case;
(v) the party against whom the judgment is sought to be recognized has been deprived, due to the actions of a foreign authority, of the opportunity to participate in the foreign proceedings, in particular, if summons or other actions initiating legal proceedings have not been properly served on such party. The court shall not investigate whether the requirement to initiate proceedings correctly was fulfilled if the foreign judgment was properly served on such party and the party failed to make an appeal against that foreign judgment or the party stated that it does not insist on fulfilment of this requirement;
(vi) a final decision on the same matter has been previously issued by a Slovak court or a final foreign decision on the same matter has already been recognized in the Slovak Republic or complies with the requirements of the Slovak Republic for its recognition;
(vii) recognition would be contrary to public policy in the Slovak Republic.

Arbitration

[286] A foreign arbitral award or decision of an arbitral tribunal will be recognized and enforced in Slovakia in accordance with, and subject to, the New York Convention on Recognition and Enforcement of Foreign Arbitral Awards made at New York on 10 June 1958.

SPECIFIC RULES ON PUBLIC TAKEOVERS

General

[287] Takeover offers are regulated by the Securities Act. The Securities Act implements Directive 2004/25/ES on takeover bids. The National Bank of Slovakia has competence to oversee the compliance with rules on public takeovers.

[288] Takeover offers have been rarely used for acquiring control over companies in Slovakia. Most often, controlling stakes in companies are transferred in privately negotiated deals or in tenders organized by the government in the process of privatization of state-owned property.

[289] Accordingly, although the legislative framework for public takeovers exists, its application in practice is very limited.

Applicability of Takeover Provisions in the Securities Act

[290] The Securities Act applies to takeover offers in respect of (i) shares; (ii) temporary share certificates that substitute shares; and (iii) other transferrable securities; carrying voting rights and admitted to trading on the regulated market in Slovakia or in the EEA.

[291] A takeover offer is defined as a public offer to purchase or exchange all or some of the shares of a company, addressed to shareholders of this company. The Securities Act recognizes a mandatory takeover and a voluntary takeover offer.

The Takeover Offer Process

[292] The takeover offer process is rather formalized and its main steps are as follows:

(i) takeover offer notice by an offeror to the target company's board of directors and the National Bank of Slovakia;
(ii) takeover offer proposal submitted to the National Bank of Slovakia (for the sake of completeness please note that partial offers are also possible. There

shall be no exclusivity for the offeror. The terms of the takeover offer shall be the same for all shareholders);

(iii) takeover offer proceeding before the National Bank of Slovakia; and

(iv) acceptance of the takeover offer by the National Bank of Slovakia.

Rules for Buying the Shares During a Proposal

[293] If between the disclosure of a takeover and the end of its validity, the offeror or a person acting in concert with it acquires any shares of the target for a consideration greater than that offered under the approved offer, the offeror shall raise the offered consideration so that it is not lower than the highest consideration provided for the acquisition of the target's shares.

Withdrawal of Takeover Offer

[294] Takeover offer may be withdrawn only if this is expressly provided for in the offer, the conditions laid by the Securities Act are met, and the grounds for withdrawal arose independent of the will of the offeror or persons acting in concert with it. A takeover offer may not be withdrawn if it has already been accepted by any addressee. The withdrawal is subject to the approval of the National Bank of Slovakia.

Breakthrough Rule

[295] The breakthrough rule stipulates that the restrictions on:

(i) the transfer of shares provided for in (a) the articles of association of the target company; (b) contractual agreements between the target company and its shareholders; or (c) mutual agreements between shareholders; can be overridden in respect of the offeror by decision of the general meeting; and

(ii) voting rights at the target company's general meeting of shareholders, which decides on any defensive measures provided for in (a) the articles of association; (b) contractual agreements between the target company and its shareholders; or (c) mutual agreements between shareholders; can be overridden by decision of the general meeting.

[296] All entities whose rights directly ensuing from the articles of association of the target company or contractual agreements have been affected by the application of the breakthrough rule must be indemnified.

Defence Tactics and Duties of the Board of Directors

[297] Many defence tactics used in the course of takeover battles, in particular those used in the United States (US) or the UK, may not be legal or feasible in Slovakia.

[298] From the time the members of the board of directors or the supervisory board of the target company receive offeror's takeover offer above, they must not pass any measures or take any actions that could prevent the addressees of the takeover offer from knowing the relevant facts and deciding freely on the takeover offer unless:

(i) such particular acts and measures are approved by the general meeting of the target company in advance, during the time allowed for acceptance of the offer; or
(ii) the act is made or the measure is taken in the course of the target company's regular business operations.

[299] Members of the board of directors or the supervisory board of the target company may seek a competing takeover offer and may do so even without approval of the general meeting. A competing takeover offer may also be made by the members of the board of directors or the supervisory board themselves.

Mandatory Takeover Offer

[300] An entity whose shareholding exceeds 33% of all voting rights related to the shares issued by the target company (the '**Decisive Share**') must make a mandatory takeover offer. Until the mandatory takeover offer is made public, the shareholder holding the Decisive Share may not exercise any voting rights in the target company exceeding the Decisive Share. Such shareholder is required to make mandatory offer both in situations when the Decisive Share was exceeded individually by that shareholder or collectively with cooperating entities.

Consideration

[301] Consideration may be paid up in money or in securities or as a combination of both of these forms. If a part of the consideration is offered as securities, the offeror must also offer, as an alternative, the consideration in money.

[302] The consideration must further correspond to the value of shares in the target company. Fair consideration must be proved by an appraiser's report.

Squeeze-Out

[303] An offeror holding shares representing at least 95% of the registered capital and the voting rights in the target company has the right to squeeze-out the holders of the remaining shares. To squeeze-out means to require all holders of the remaining shares to sell those shares for a fair consideration.

[304] The offeror must notify the National Bank of Slovakia, the target company and the remaining shareholders of his or her decision to squeeze them out, and of circumstances under which he or she acquired this right. The squeeze-out right takes effect towards the remaining shareholders only with the consent of the National Bank of Slovakia.

Sell-Out

[305] Should relevant circumstances allowing the offeror to perform the squeeze-out, holders of the remaining shares also have the right to sell to the offeror those shares for a fair consideration.

Sanctions

[306] Should the National Bank of Slovakia determine any breach of laws in the acting of the offeror preparing and filing the takeover offer, competing takeover offer, mandatory takeover offer and/or application of the squeeze-out right, it is entitled to:

(i) impose respective measures with the aim to eliminate the breach;
(ii) impose a fine of up to EUR5 000 000 or a fine of up to EUR10 000 000 an din certain cases up to 10% of the total yearly turnover of the offeror in case of repeating breach of laws;
(iii) order the publication of corrected incomplete, incorrect or untrue information that were published under an obligation imposed by law;
(iv) suspend the takeover offer, competing takeover offer, mandatory takeover offer and execution of the squeeze-out right;
(v) ban the takeover offer, competing takeover offer, mandatory takeover offer and execution of the squeeze-out right; and/or
(vi) impose on those members of target company's board of directors who breached the law a fine of up to EUR5 000 000 or a temporary ban to exercise the office of a member of a board of directors, or impose a fine of up to EUR10 000 000 and a permanent ban to exercise the office of a member of a board of directors in case of repeating breach of law.

OTHER RELEVANT LAWS

Anti-bribery/Anti-corruption Laws

[307] The law broadly recognizes five different crimes of corruption – passive bribery, active bribery, indirect bribery, elections bribery and sports bribery. Crimes of corruption need not to be committed by or against public officials. Instead, crimes of corruption can be committed by any person (irrespective of its status or position/office).

[308] Public officials are subject to stricter criminal liability. The fact that the crime of corruption is committed by or against the public officials results in the aggravation of the criminal liability/sanctions on the offender imposed by the Criminal Code.

[309] As a general safeguard, however, criminal liability of public officials under the relevant provisions of the Criminal Code (including the criminal liability for crimes of corruption) require that the offence be committed in connection with the exercise of their powers and responsibilities. In other words, it is not sufficient that the person is expressly designated as public official but such public official must commit the offence exercising the powers and responsibilities of the public official. Hence the criminal liability is not connected with the status of a person but rather with an activity of such person.

[310] In practice, however, despite relatively good anti-bribery/anti-corruption laws, the bribery and corruption largely goes unnoticed or is not properly investigated.

[311] In addition, Slovakia has Anti-Money Laundering Act which sets out the rules against money laundering and terrorism financing.

[312] Where US or other international investors that are subject to the Foreign Corrupt Practices Act (FCPA) or UK Bribery Act are involved in M&A transactions, they may ask for particular representations or provisions indicating that Slovak counterparts have not engaged in any actions that would violate such laws. Generally, however, such laws have not had a noticeable impact on M&A transactions in Slovakia. For completeness, however, we note that there are FCPA investigations in Slovakia that include the Slovak subsidiaries of the US companies – to our knowledge none of them is directly related to M&A activity.

Intellectual Property Rights

[313] The Industrial Property Office maintains registers of registered patents, utility models ('small patents'), designs, trademarks, designations of origin, geographical indications and topographies of semiconductor products.

[314] Application forms are available online and although can be submitted electronically, the Industrial Property Office will still require paper versions to be sent

by post. The application process is relatively straightforward. The Industrial Property Office also accepts applications to the international or European registers.

[315] Online versions of registers are available, however, these have only informative character. Therefore, intellectual property rights for due diligence purposes can be easily verified via official extracts which can be requested from the Office for an administrative fee.

[316] The Industrial Property Office only handles application disputes regarding the priority rights. Enforcement of intellectual property rights is therefore subject to normal court proceedings. District Court in Banska Bystrica has special competence to hear the disputes from intellectual property in Slovakia at first instance. The appeal court for such disputes is the Regional court in Banska Bystrica.

[317] We note that transfers of intellectual property rights should also be registered with the Industrial Property Office. While a failure to register a transfer does not render such a transfer invalid, such a transfer would not be effective against third parties (e.g. any claims for infringement would have to be brought by the original rights holder).

Change of Control Clauses

[318] The 'change of control' clauses are enforceable and are commonly used in many types of contracts. Typically 'change of control' clauses would form part of the banking loan arrangements of the target company.

[319] When undertaking due diligence in connection with an acquisition, the 'change of control' clauses are key issue to look for so that such issues can be addressed by the parties before completing the M&A transaction.

THE DUE DILIGENCE PROCESS

General

[320] Purchasers carry out investigation of the legal, financial, technological and environmental position of a target, and all relevant and related circumstances.

[321] Legal due diligence is generally prepared once the seller has committed to sell the target and the purchaser has decided to acquire the target, often by signing a 'letter of intent', or has submitted a preliminary non-binding offer based on initial information provided by the seller and has, based on such offer, been granted exclusivity for negotiations with the seller for a certain period of time. At this stage, all related and relevant legal relations, the validity of existing agreements and other legal matters must be clarified so that a final decision in respect of the acquisition may be taken.

Specific Issues to Be Reviewed

[322] When acquiring a Slovak company whose (or its legal predecessor's) history goes back before 1990, any assets of such company or assets acquired from such company, special attention should be paid to reviewing the accuracy of the privatization processes. This requirement applies especially in relation to the ownership of shares in such company, its real estate and intellectual property rights. Due to the hectic nature of the times, the lack of experience and the ambiguity of laws valid at the time, some of the privatizations of state property, especially those in the beginning of the 1990, were not performed properly. Some of the mistakes that occurred during the privatization process might still have a material adverse effect on an acquisition carried out now.

[323] In real estate transactions or other M&A transactions where real estate plays crucial role, title check to land covering its acquisition history over ten years before closing the transaction, should be performed. This may be rather costly and time-consuming, taking into account imperfect historical records in the Real Estate Register and number of unknown owners of (in particular) agricultural land.

Disclosure Restriction

General

[324] Generally, even the majority shareholder (a seller) is not entitled to order the target company to provide any information to a third party (a purchaser) for the purpose of a due diligence review, unless it is allowed to do so under the Memorandum/Articles of Association of the target company or the target company forms part of a declared concern. Therefore, any due diligence process requires cooperation with the representatives of both the seller and the target company as the representatives of the target company are solely responsible for its business management and are obliged to act in its best interest, i.e. independently from its shareholders, whose interests may differ from those of the company.

[325] During due diligence, certain documents and items of information are disclosed to the purchaser and/or its professional advisors. In doing so, various legal restrictions must be observed. Thus, an investor will only gain access to certain kinds of information (as defined below) when committing itself to comply with security measures adopted by the target company to avoid the abuse or disclosure of such information by the purchaser or its professional advisors. Such measures are commonly set out in the form of a confidentiality agreement concluded between the target company and the purchaser/its professional advisors and in the form of binding data room rules.

Business Secret

[326] A business secret includes information that is not commonly available in business community, is related to the target company, has certain value or potential value and that its holder requires to be kept confidential. In the course of due diligence, a reviewer will usually encounter business secrets of the target company as well as business secrets of the entities in contractual (or other) relationships with the target company.

[327] It is at the sole discretion of the target company whether business secrets shall be disclosed to the purchaser and to decide the terms and conditions for such disclosure. This freedom of disclosure is not absolute as the parties are still bound by the restrictions stipulated by the Competition Act. Disclosure of business secrets during due diligence shall not result in a prohibited information exchange between competitors on either a horizontal or vertical level which could lead to distortion of competition.

[328] In relation to information classified as a business secret by third parties, unless the third party consented to data disclosure, the target company shall ensure a level of protection corresponding to the scope of protection it owes to the respective third party.

Personal Data Protection

[329] Personal data means any information relating to an identified or identifiable individual, defined as a 'data subject' (not applicable to data concerning legal entities). The target company is only entitled to disclose personal data upon the consent of the relevant data subject or in cases where an exemption is stipulated under the GDPR.

[330] There is no explicit exemption for the disclosure of personal data within the scope of due diligence. However, it is the prevailing view that such disclosure is allowed provided that the disclosure is essential for the protection of the rights of the target company. Generally, in the event of any disclosure of personal data, adequate protection of the data subject's private and personal life must always be ensured.

Banking Secret

[331] Under the Banking Act, all information on banking transactions and financial services of banks, including account balances and deposits, shall be the subject of a banking secret. This applies to information concerning both individuals and legal entities.

[332] Generally, a bank is prohibited from providing information considered a banking secret without its customers' consent unless a specific exemption provided by the Banking Act stipulates otherwise. Under the Banking Act, information containing banking secret can only be provided, in relation to a potential sale of the bank, under a prior written consent of the National Bank of Slovakia. Such information can only be provided to the purchaser or its advisors which are, by operation of the Banking Act, subject to confidentiality obligation. Notwithstanding the foregoing, the National Bank of Slovakia shall not issue its consent unless the target bank enters into a specific non-disclosure agreement with the purchaser and each of its advisors which are to have access to information containing banking secret.

[333] In order to mitigate any regulatory or competition law risks, it is strongly recommended that the reports prepared by the professional advisors for the purchaser shall contain information in an anonymous or aggregate form only (i.e. without disclosing the identity of the bank's client).

Other Restrictions

[334] Restrictions similar to those relating to banking secrets apply to information on the insurance policies of both individuals and corporate entities pursuant to the Insurance Act and pension insurance policies under the Pension Funds Act.

[335] A specific confidentiality duty relates to information affecting the legitimate interest of an investment company, investment fund or shareholders and trustees under the Collective Investment Act.

[336] The Capital Markets Act imposes a general confidentiality duty on certain entities with respect to information that could potentially be important for the assessment of the trends on the capital markets or potentially harm an entity using the services rendered on the capital markets before such information was made public.

ROLE OF THE COURTS

General

[337] The Slovak courts are organized hierarchically (District Courts, Regional Courts and the Supreme Court). Separate Constitutional Court rules on the conflicts between laws and interprets the Constitution.

[338] The courts are generally neutral and do not tend to support domestic residents and companies over foreigners nor individuals over businesses; however on instances, the courts tend to lean in favour of one party, such instances being in particular consumers and employee disputes.

[339] The level of independence of the courts lags significantly; Amnesty International is consistently ranking Slovak courts at the worst positions in worldwide courts' independence rating.

[340] The amount of expenses and laboriousness reaches the standards of the majority of the European justice systems. However, the length of the proceedings at the courts is significantly above the standard European levels.

[341] For example, the average time to resolve commercial dispute is 21.6 months and civil law dispute is 20.8 months (data for 2017). However, there is a great number of disputes that drag into number of years, even decades.

Alternative Dispute Settlement Methods

[342] Given the practice of courts, sophisticated parties tend to choose alternative dispute settlement methods instead of general courts. Arbitration is the preferred method of alternative dispute resolution. Mediation and other methods are not much developed in Slovakia.

[343] In general, the parties are free to decide whether to use the general courts or arbitration. Exclusive jurisdiction of courts is laid down in certain narrow instances; such as in case of disputes relating to the origination, change or termination of ownership right or other property rights to the real estate, related with the bankruptcy.

[344] Arbitration proceedings in Slovakia are regulated by two arbitration acts: (i) the Commercial Arbitration Act which is based on the United Nations Commission on International Trade Law (UNCITRAL) Model Law and regulates domestic and international commercial arbitration in Slovakia, and (ii) Consumer Arbitration Act, which is designed for the consumer arbitration and is strictly regulated. The parties in commercial arbitration are free to decide that the arbitration proceedings are to take place in Slovakia or elsewhere. On the other hand, the Slovak consumer disputes in arbitration can be heard and decided only before the licensed arbitration courts in Slovakia.

[345] The domestic arbitration bodies lack recognition. The Arbitration Court of the Slovak Bar Association however commenced the way to became reliable domestic arbitration institution. It is therefore common to arbitrate the disputes involving Slovak party before international arbitration institutions such as the Vienna International Arbitration Centre (VIAC), International Chamber of Commerce (ICC) and the like.

Enforceability of Key Contractual Provisions

[346] The law provides for a freedom of choice and contractual provisions are generally enforceable; certain exceptions nonetheless apply such as:

- courts may not give effect to any indemnity for legal costs incurred by a litigant, irrespective if such indemnity is agreed between the parties;
- courts may refuse to grant a claim for damages, if an act or omission of the claimant has caused the damages (either partly or entirely) or if the claimant failed to comply with its statutory obligation to mitigate the damages.

[347] Generally, restrictive covenants (preventing the vendors competing with the business sold) are enforceable. Such restrictive covenants however must comply with the general EU competition rules.

[348] Enforcement of warranty or indemnity of claims are possible despite the fact that the courts are not particularly experienced when it comes to deal with the issues of indemnity and warranty claims. In this sense, the arbitration seems to be much more favourable given the experience of arbitrators with the indemnity and warranty claims.

MERGER CONTROL

General Introduction

[349] The core rules of the Slovak competition law, including those dealing with merger control, are laid down in the Competition Act that has been in effect from 1 May 2001. Following the accession of the Slovak Republic to the EU on 1 May 2004, the Competition Act has undergone significant changes and it currently complies with the EU competition law system. The authority responsible for the enforcement of competition law is the Slovak Antimonopoly Office (the 'Competition Authority').

Merger Control Test

[350] A transaction must be notified to the Competition Authority if the following three conditions are met:

(i) the transaction constitutes a concentration;
(ii) at least one of the turnover thresholds is met; and
(iii) the transaction is not subject to notification to the Commission under Council Regulation No. 139/2004 on the control of concentrations between undertakings (the 'ECMR').

Concentration

[351] The following transactions constitute concentrations within the meaning of the Competition Act:

(i) merger of two or more independent undertakings by acquisition or by formation of a new company (amalgamation);
(ii) acquisition of direct or indirect control by one or more undertakings over an undertaking or its part (or assets) by:
   - acquisition of securities (such as shares), ownership or membership interests;

- establishment of a (full-function) joint venture;
- agreement (such as shareholder agreements, memoranda of association, articles of association, controlling agreements, licence agreements, loan agreements); or
- any other manner that allows the exercise of decisive influence over another undertaking or its part (or assets).

[352] In contrast, the transactions stipulated above do not constitute a concentration as defined in the Competition Act if they take place between undertakings belonging to the same group. Such intra-group consolidations or reorganizations are exempted from the notification obligation to the Competition Authority. In addition, certain transactions performed by investment entities (e.g., banks, securities brokers and other financial institutions) do not constitute a concentration and are not subject to notification to the Competition Authority.

[353] Two or more concentrations which are individually not subject to clearance by the Competition Authority and which occur within two years between the same undertakings and are jointly subject to clearance by the Competition Authority are considered a single concentration.

Turnover Thresholds

[354] The turnover condition is satisfied if one of the following thresholds is met:

(i) combined aggregate turnover of the undertakings concerned in the Slovak Republic is at least EUR46 m for the closed accounting period preceding the concentration, and at least two of the parties to the concentration generated turnover of at least EUR14 m each in the Slovak Republic for the closed accounting period preceding the concentration; or

(ii) total turnover attained in the Slovak Republic for the closed accounting period preceding the concentration:
   - if the concentration is a merger or amalgamation of two or more independent undertakings, by at least one undertaking concerned was at least EUR14 m and, at the same time, another undertaking concerned had a worldwide aggregate turnover of at least EUR46 m in the closed accounting period preceding the concentration; or
   - if the concentration is an acquisition of sole or joint control, by the undertaking concerned over which control is being acquired, was at least EUR14 m and, at the same time, another undertaking concerned had a worldwide aggregate turnover of at least EUR46 m in the closed accounting period preceding the concentration; or
   - if the concentration is the creation of a joint venture, by at least one undertaking concerned was at least EUR14 m and, at the same time, another undertaking concerned had a worldwide aggregate turnover of at least EUR46 m for the closed accounting period preceding the concentration.

[355] The Competition Act also provides detailed rules for calculation of the turnovers.

Transaction Subject to EU Merger Control Rules

[356] Even if a transaction qualifies as a concentration and one of the turnover thresholds is met, it does not need to be notified to the Competition Authority if it must be notified to the Commission under the ECMR. In such case a 'one-stop shop' principle applies and the transaction is reviewed by the Commission only.

Notification Procedure

[357] If all three of the above conditions are met, the transaction is subject to notification to, and clearance by, the Competition Authority. This section deals with proceedings before the Competition Authority.

Filing Undertakings

[358] The following undertakings are required to file a notification (and are liable for failure to file a notification):

Merger by acquisition or by formation of a new company	All the concentrating undertakings (notification is to be made jointly)
Acquisition of control over another undertaking or its part	Undertaking acquiring control
Establishment of a joint venture	All of the undertakings establishing joint control over the undertaking (notification must be made jointly)
Takeover bid	The undertaking proposing the takeover bid
Public tender	The selected bidder in the public tender

Opening of Merger Proceedings

[359] Merger proceedings are opened after the Competition Authority receives a notification of concentration, or at the Competition Authority's own initiative. There is no deadline for submitting the notification, however the concentration must be notified to the Competition Authority before the rights and obligations resulting from the concentration are exercised and after:

(i) an agreement is concluded;

(ii) acceptance of a bid in a public tender is announced;
(iii) decision of a public authority is delivered to the undertaking;
(iv) an announcement of an acquisition bid;
(v) the date when the Commission informed the undertaking that the Competition Authority will deal with the matter; or
(vi) the date of occurrence of other fact/circumstance giving rise to concentration.

[360] Until the concentration is approved by the Competition Authority, the undertakings concerned are prohibited from implementing the concentration. The notification may also take place prior to the conclusion of an agreement or prior to another event establishing the concentration described above, provided that the notified concentration is subject to merger proceedings by the Competition Authority. Such early notification shall contain written reasoning and evidence confirming the above.

[361] The Competition Authority announces the opening of the proceedings in the Commercial Bulletin and on its website.

Notification

[362] In the notification, the notifying undertakings must provide the Competition Authority with extensive information about the concentration. The scope of documents and other information that must be provided to the Competition Authority is primarily as follows:

(i) the official form for concentration notifications (Form CO) or simplified concentration notification (short Form CO);
(ii) powers of attorney (if the concentrating undertakings are represented in the proceedings by attorney-at-law or by other agent). If the representative is a legal person, the PoA must specify the person to act on behalf of the issuer;
(iii) extracts from the Commercial Register for each of the undertakings concerned or, if the undertakings are not Slovak entities, from other equivalent register. If the undertakings are not Slovak entities, the extract must be apostilled/superlegalized (unless an international treaty between Slovakia and the respective third country waives this obligation);
(iv) by-laws and articles of association of the undertakings concerned;
(v) document(s) establishing the concentration of the undertakings concerned;
(vi) annual reports and audited financial statements of the undertakings concerned for the last financial year;
(vii) reports, analyses, studies and other similar documents that have been prepared for members of the Board of Directors or Supervisory Board (or of any other similar corporate body) or for shareholders' meeting in order to assess the concentration;
(viii) minutes from General Meetings, Minutes from Board meetings, Supervisory Boards, management or other body related to the concentration;

(ix) reports, analyses, studies and other similar documents dated no sooner than two years prior to the concentration, that include information for purposes of market analysis in relation to market shares, competition on the market, competing undertakings and potential of sales growth or expansion to further product or geographic markets;
(x) affidavit to the effect that all details provided in the notification of concentration are true, accurate and complete and that originals, true and full copies of documents are provided and that all estimates provided are the best estimates based on underlying data and that the issuer is aware of the consequences of submitting incomplete, incorrect or untrue information or documents;
(xi) proof of payment of the administrative fee of EUR5 000;
(xii) the official form for concentration notifications excluding trade secrets and confidential information;
(xiii) concentration notification on an electronic data carrier;
(xiv) the documents must be in Slovak. If originals are not in Slovak, their translation, or at least the translation of their relevant parts, must also be submitted.

[363] The core notification document is the questionnaire referred to in point (i); it is based on the European Form CO. It requires an extensive scope of information (such as information about the undertakings concerned; description of the concentration; information about any links in terms of capital or financial holding; information on the connection through personnel; information on affected markets, etc.).

[364] The Competition Authority has issued detailed guidelines regarding the application of the merger control rules.

[365] Following a reasoned request of the notifying party, the Competition Authority may reduce the scope of the information required. If during the proceedings, the Competition Authority ascertains that the reduced scope of information is not sufficient to allow adopting a decision on the matter, the Authority may request additional information and documents.

Stages of the Proceedings

Notification and Time Limits

[366] The Competition Authority issues its decision within twenty-five working days following the date of receipt of the complete notification of concentration. If the notification is incomplete, the twenty-five working day period is resting from the day the Competition Authority requests the notifying party in writing to complete the notification, until the day the notifying party submits a complete concentration notification. The Competition Authority typically delivers a simplified reasoning for its decision. When adopting a decision with a simplified reasoning, the Competition Authority will not ask the parties to submit their observations before the final decision is issued.

[367] In case the Competition Authority is dealing with a concentration requiring more detailed analyses of the relevant market and/or has competition concerns, the decision on concentration is issued in ninety working days (phase 2) following the date of delivery of a decision on moving proceedings to phase 2 to the notifying party. The Competition Authority informs the notifying party about this within twenty-five working days.

[368] Upon a reasoned request by a party, or with such party's consent, the Competition Authority may extend the time limits for issuing the decision on concentration prior to their expiry as appropriate, and even repeatedly, by up to thirty working days in aggregate.

Assessment

[369] The Competition Authority assesses whether the transaction does significantly impede effective competition on the relevant market, in particular as a result of creation or strengthening of a dominant position.

[370] The assessment of effects of a concentration on competition is made, in particular, in view of the following: necessity to preserve and further develop effective competition, structure of all markets affected by the concentration, market shares of the undertakings concerned in such markets, their economic and financial power, legal and other barriers to entry by other entities in the markets, alternatives available to suppliers and consumers, development of supply and demand in the markets, needs and interests of consumers, research and development.

[371] Provided that the concentration does not significantly impede effective competition on the relevant market, in particular as a result of creation or strengthening of a dominant position, the Competition Authority will approve the concentration.

[372] On the other hand, if the Competition Authority concludes that the concentration significantly impedes effective competition on the relevant market, in particular as a result of creation or strengthening of a dominant position or coordination of competition behaviour, it will prohibit the concentration.

Commitments

[373] Where the Competition Authority has concerns about a notified concentration, it may clear the concentration on certain terms and conditions defined in the clearance (the 'Commitments'). The Competition Authority will request the relevant party to propose and reason, in writing, Commitments within thirty working days of the request, and may extend this period of time if deemed appropriate.

Implementation of the Transaction

Mandatory Suspension of Implementation

[374] The Competition Act provides that the undertakings concerned are prohibited from implementing a transaction until it is approved by the Competition Authority. The undertakings must mainly avoid influencing each other's competitive conduct (e.g. they must refrain from exercise of voting rights, adoption of new business plans, change of executives or taking any other action that may materially affect their businesses or operations). However, this does not apply to concentrations in the form of takeover offers or a series of transactions with publicly traded securities, all provided that there is no delay in notification and no exercise of voting rights connected with such securities until the concentration is approved by the Competition Authority.

Application for an Exemption

[375] The concentrating undertakings may apply to the Competition Authority, either at the time of filing the standard form notification or in the course of notification proceedings, for an exemption from ban on implementation of the transaction. The applicant must back such application with relevant/serious reasons.

[376] The Competition Authority will adopt a decision on the application within twenty working days following its submission.

[377] If the Competition Authority grants an exemption, it may require certain commitments it may consider necessary for preserving effective competition.

Premature Implementation

[378] If the Competition Authority ascertains that the concentrating undertakings implemented the transaction without filing the notification or prior to its approval, it is authorized, in addition to the imposition of fines described below, to order the undertakings to restore the level of competition as existed prior to establishment of concentration, especially to order 'demerger', that is, to sell the shares, transfer the business, cancel any relevant agreements and/or adopt other measures necessary to restore effective competition in the relevant market.

[379] Also, if undertakings fail to carry out the commitments set out in the clearance decision, the Competition Authority may repeal the clearance and prohibit the concentration. The Competition Authority may also change or repeal a clearance decision if information provided in the proceedings was false or incomplete, or if the concentration was carried out in otherwise than as notified. However, the Competition Authority may waive or change some of the commitments where there is substantial change in the relevant market or a claim by an undertaking that there are serious reasons for non-compliance with some of its commitments.

Competition Authority's Rights

Right to Information

[380] In general, it is in the undertakings' interest to provide the Competition Authority with sufficient information about the transaction so that the proceedings are smooth and as short as possible.

[381] The Competition Authority may also request additional information from undertakings. Failure to provide the required information may result in stay of the proceedings. The Competition Authority may also impose severe fines for failure to submit such information.

Power to Investigate

[382] The Competition Authority has extensive powers to investigate undertakings in the Slovak Republic, including the right to enter business premises and land, to make copies or extracts from books or records, to require explanations or seal off any business premises and books or records while an inspection is underway. Acting on a prior court authorization, the Competition Authority may even inspect private premises, including the homes of directors, managers and other employees of the undertakings concerned.

Fines and Remedial Measures

Fines

[383] The Competition Authority may impose severe fines for breach of the merger control regulations. These fines may amount up to:

(i) 10% of the turnover attained in the last financial year, if there was a breach of the obligation to notify the transaction to the Competition Authority prior to implementing the transaction, or if the transaction has been implemented without, or under pending approval by the Competition Authority (unless the Competition Authority grants an exception), or if the undertaking failed to carry out other enforceable decision of the Competition Authority;

(ii) 1% of the turnover attained in the last financial period, or EUR1 650 for a natural person who is not an entrepreneur, if the information requested by the Competition Authority was not filed within the set time, or if the information filed was incomplete or false, or if the undertaking denied the examination of documents by the Competition Authority;

(iii) 1% of the turnover attained in the last financial period of an undertaking which was having its premises or vehicles investigated, or was supposed to have them investigated, if the undertaking denied to cooperate with the employees of the Competition Authority in the course of an ongoing investigation, or if the undertaking did not enable its employees to provide explanations to the Competition Authority, or failed to provide the Competition Authority with documents necessary for its activities, or failed to ensure access to all documents, information and data in electronic form; if the above investigation was being conducted under a court order, a fine of up to EUR25 000 may be imposed;

(iv) 5% of the turnover attained in the last financial period of an undertaking which was having its premises or vehicles investigated, or was supposed to have them investigated, if the undertaking failed to ensure access to its premises or vehicles, open closed premises and their equipment, or otherwise ensure access to documents or data carriers on which the information is recorded, or if the undertaking failed to ensure that the seal on sealed documents, data carriers on which the information is recorded, sealed premises or vehicles is not broken; if the above investigation was being conducted under a court order, a fine of up to EUR80 000 may be imposed; and

(v) EUR3 300 for not attending an oral hearing without serious reasons, not notifying the Competition Authority of any changes in proceedings or changes in the registered office or permanent residence of the undertakings concerned, not notifying the change of the person authorized to accept documents on behalf of the undertakings concerned, or not notifying the occurrence of any other event necessary for due delivery of documents, or other obstruction of proceedings.

[384] If an undertaking, or a legal person that is not an undertaking, that generated turnover of no more than EUR330, or generated no turnover whatsoever or its turnover cannot be calculated, acts as described in (ii), (iii) and (iv) above, the Competition Authority shall impose a fine of up to EUR330 000; however, this shall not apply in case of court-ordered investigations.

[385] Fines may be imposed repeatedly. Fines may be imposed four years after the opening of the proceedings and/or eight years after the breach; otherwise, the statute of limitations will apply.

Remedial Measures

[386] In addition to the above fines, the Competition Authority may impose remedial measures and may set reasonable time limits for their implementation. For instance, the Competition Authority may order that the undertakings demerge or take other steps required to restore the effective competition on the relevant market.

TAXATION

The Slovak Tax System

[387] Below we provide an overview of taxes applicable to Slovak businesses and a brief description of income taxes, value-added tax and certain fundamental considerations in structuring M&A transaction from tax perspective.

[388] Currently, the Slovak tax system comprises the following taxes:

(i) income taxes (corporate income tax and personal income tax);
(ii) value added tax (VAT);
(iii) excise duties;
(iv) energy taxes;
(v) real estate tax; and
(vi) tax on vehicles.

Corporate Tax

[389] Slovak tax residents, that is, companies with their seat or place of management in Slovakia, are taxed on their worldwide income. Non-Slovak tax residents are taxed only on their income from Slovak sources, such as interest, royalties or permanent establishment income flowing from Slovakia while respecting the provisions of applicable double taxation treaties. Slovakia is party to over fifty double taxation treaties. Most of the treaties are based on the 1977 Organisation for Economic Co-operation and Development (OECD) Model Convention.

[390] The corporate income tax rate is 21%.

[391] The tax base is the profit (or loss) reported according to Slovak Accounting Standards, adjusted for non-deductible expenses and non-taxable income, as set out in Act No. 595/2003 on Income Taxes, as amended (the '**Income Tax Act**'). Businesses who prepare their financial statements in IAS must convert their IAS profit/loss to Slovak Accounting Standards to arrive at the corporate income tax base.

[392] Tax losses may be carried forward and set off against future profits in subsequent four years. Companies within the same group are generally unable to transfer losses to each other for tax purposes, which is because under the Income Tax Act a tax loss is not transferable and no grouping is possible.

The distribution of profits (dividends) is subject to withholding tax as follows:

- **No tax**: dividends paid/received by legal entities resident in Slovakia or in a treaty state.
- **35%**: dividends paid to legal entities or individuals resident in a non-treaty state or dividends received by Slovak residents from a legal entity in a non-treaty state.
- **7%:** dividends paid to individuals resident in Slovakia or in a treaty state or dividends received by individuals resident in Slovakia from a treaty state.

[393] 'Treaty states' are listed on the Ministry of Finance website, namely states that have signed a double taxation treaty or similar to the Slovak Republic.

[394] New thin capitalization rules have been introduced recently in the tax system. In brief, tax deductibility of interest on related party loans is limited to 25% of EBITDA declared by the debtor in the fiscal year in question.

Personal Income Tax and Social Security

[395] Personal income tax is levied at two rates: 19% on income up to certain annual threshold (in July 2019 this threshold is approximately EUR37 000 and it may be adjusted annually) and 25% on income exceeding the threshold. The tax is levied on the gross income of employees, net income of entrepreneurs, capital income and other extraordinary income of private individuals. The tax year is always the calendar year.

[396] In addition, the employment income and income of self-employed entrepreneurs is subject to social security and health insurance contributions. Contributions on employment income are shared between employees and employers at the approximate rate of 1:3 and represent together approximately 50% of gross income (that is, employer pays some 35% and employee 15% of gross income). Annual contributions are no longer capped as in the past.

[397] Dividends received by individuals are subject to the 7 % or 35 % withholding tax as per the overview provided in paragraph **[389]–[394]** above.

VAT

[398] VAT legislation has been harmonized with EU Directives as of 1 May 2004.

[399] The standard VAT rate is 20%; the reduced VAT rate is 10% but applies only to a limited range of goods.

[400] In general, a business must register for VAT if its turnover for VAT purposes during any consecutive twelve months exceeds EUR50 000. It may also have to register for VAT if it purchases goods from other EU Member States or certain services from abroad. The buyer must also automatically register where he or she acquires an enterprise from a seller who is VAT-registered.

[401] Voluntary VAT registration and VAT group registrations are also possible.

Other Relevant Taxes on Transactions or Ownership

[402] There are no transfer taxes (such as e.g. real estate transfer tax or gift tax) and no capital duties in Slovakia.

[403] Companies and individuals who own property as at 1 January of the current year are subject to real estate tax in that year. The tax base is determined on the basis of area and deemed value of plots of land and the rates are determined annually by municipalities and can vary significantly depending on the region. Real estate taxes may have significant influence on real estate transactions but are normally insignificant in other types of M&A.

Structuring the Investment: Withholding Taxes

[404] Until 2017, there was no tax on received or paid dividends in Slovakia, which made the country a good location for certain investments, in particular for locating holding companies. This is no longer applicable, however certain benefits of the tax-free system still remain (as described in paragraph **[389]–[394]** above) and the wide network of double tax treaties still makes Slovakia and interesting jurisdiction for structuring investments. Capital gains are unfortunately subject to personal or corporate tax (as applicable) and no participation exemption is available. Exit strategy must, therefore, be planned carefully, using vehicles located in more favourable jurisdictions that offer participation exemption or similar beneficial regime.

[405] Interest paid to a non-Slovak tax resident is generally subject to a 19% withholding tax unless a double taxation treaty sets out otherwise. Also, the withholding tax on interest charged between related entities can generally be eliminated on conditions set out in the EU Interest-Royalties Directive. Identical rules apply to royalties.

[406] Withholding tax of 35% is levied on the most types of income (including e.g., management and service fees) if they are paid to a resident of a state with which Slovakia has no double taxation treaty or no tax cooperation/exchange of information treaty.

Tax Considerations Arising on M&A Transactions

Asset Sale

[407] Any profit from the sale of assets is added to the seller's regular business profits and is, therefore, subject to income tax. On the other hand, a loss from the sale of land (not buildings) is not tax deductible.

[408] A 'step-up' in the tax base of assets is achieved as the assets are depreciated in the buyer's books from the acquisition price as if they were newly acquired. Certain assets, such as land, are excluded from depreciation.

[409] Interest on acquisition financing is, in general, tax deductible. However, if the financing is provided by a related entity, there are restrictions set out in the transfer pricing rules.

[410] Any tax losses realized by the seller and related to the transferred assets may not be transferred to the buyer.

[411] The transfer of movable assets, construction plots (plots of land designated in the relevant zoning plan for construction) and rights is subject to VAT. The transfer of real estate (except for construction plots), executed five years or more after the issuing of a use permit or the first real use of buildings, is exempt from VAT.

[412] In the event of acquisition of assets, the corporate tax, VAT and other tax liabilities that have arisen in connection with the seller's enterprise do not pass to the buyer.

Share Sale

[413] Profit on a sale by a private individual is reported in an annual tax return and subject to personal income tax. Profit on the sale realized by a Slovak corporate resident is included in the annual corporate income tax return. A loss is, in general, tax deductible.

[414] Profit on the sale of shares/an ownership interest in a Slovak company realized by a non-resident seller may be subject to personal or corporate tax (as the case may be) in Slovakia, if not exempted under the relevant double tax treaty.

[415] The acquisition price of shares is tax deductible for the buyer upon the disposal of the shares. No 'step-up' can be achieved in the tax base of the underlying assets owned by the target since the transfer does not affect the acquisition cost.

[416] Deduction of tax losses carried forward by the transferred company is not restricted.

[417] Costs related to the holding of shares/an ownership interest (such as interest on acquisition financing) are generally tax deductible, although there are certain discussions on such deductibility. The tax deductibility of costs may also be achieved by an appropriate acquisition structuring and a subsequent transformation.

[418] The transfer of shares is subject to neither VAT nor other taxes or stamp duties.

[419] The buyer 'inherits' the tax history of the acquired company, including its latent tax liabilities. The statute of limitations is generally seven years following the end of the tax period in which the tax return in question is filed. If authorities take action with respect to a tax return before this period expires, the period is extended. The maximum statute of limitations is generally ten years, except for income tax where the statute of limitations may be extended if the taxpayer has been granted tax relief under an investment incentives programme.

Merger/De-merger

[420] From the perspective of corporate tax, the participating companies and their shareholders can decide whether hidden reserves or deficits (differences between recorded tax values and fair market values of assets and liabilities) should be realized upon transformation. If the companies decide to realize such differences, assets and liabilities are re-valued for tax purposes and the overall valuation difference has an effect on the tax base, either immediate at the time of transformation, or gradual over a period of not more than seven years (at the choice of the legal successor after transformation). If the companies decide to take over the recorded tax values of assets and liabilities from the dissolved company to its successor, no valuation differences affect the tax base.

[421] Tax loss carried forward by a dissolved company is taken over and further carried forward by its legal successor.

[422] No VAT, stamp duties or other transfer taxes are due on the transfer of assets of the dissolved company to the successor company.

[423] Tax obligations of a dissolved company pass to the legal successor on the date when the transformation was registered in the Commercial Register.

Transformation of Legal Form

[424] Transformation of a company's legal form is, in principle, tax neutral. In the tax perspective, the company maintains its continuity.

[425] Corporate income tax issues (e.g., problems with utilization of tax losses and other allowances) may appear in a situation where a limited liability company or a joint-stock company is transformed into a general partnership or a limited partnership or vice versa. This is due to different taxation of profits, as profits of partners in a general partnership and general partners in a limited partnership are not taxed at the level of the partnership but are rather allocated to the partners who report the respective profit shares in their own tax returns.

EMPLOYMENT CONSIDERATIONS

Legislative Framework

[426] Employment in the Slovak Republic is regulated by a variety of acts, of which the most important are Act No. 311/2001 the Labour Code (the '**Labour Code**'), Act No. 5/2004 on Employment Services (the '**Employment Act**'), Act No. 125/2006 on Work Inspection (the '**Inspection Act**') and Act No. 2/1991 on Collective Bargaining (the '**Collective Bargaining Act**'). EU Directives relevant to employment and cross-border posting of workers (e.g. Directive 96/71/EC and the Enforcement Directive 2014/67/EU) play an important role in shaping the above Slovak legislation.

Employment: General Concept

[427] Although the previous rigid concept of employment law has been superseded, the employment law in the Slovak Republic is still very employee-protective.

[428] Most provisions in the Labour Code are mandatory; however, parties to employment relationships may deviate from the Labour Code where the Labour Code does not prohibit so or agree on a different arrangement if the wording of the

Labour Code does not prescribe anything specific. The parties may agree on deviation(s) from the Labour Code only if the resulting arrangement(s) are more favourable to employees than the provisions of the Labour Code.

[429] The Labour Code does not distinguish between the employment of 'blue collar workers' and 'white collar workers'. All of these categories are employed under employment agreements and the rights ad remedies equally apply to all types of employees.

[430] A valid employment contract must contain the following substantial items:

(i) type of work in which the employee will be engaged and its brief characteristics;
(ii) place where the work will be performed (municipality, organizational unit or other specified place);
(iii) date on which the employee commences working;
(iv) salary conditions, unless agreed in a collective agreement.

[431] If parties do not reach an agreement on substantial arrangements of the employment, no employment contract is concluded.

[432] Employment contract must be concluded in writing and in the Slovak language. Even though the lack of written form does not render an employment contract invalid, the employer may be penalized by the relevant Work Inspectorate for a breach of the obligation to conclude written employment contracts with a fine of up to EUR100 000. Work Inspectorates are regional governmental authorities supervising compliance with the obligations arising from the labour law regulations.

[433] In addition, employer is obliged to specify in the employment contract other working conditions, such as terms of payment, working time, length of paid holiday, length of notice period, etc.

[434] If an employment contract does not contain information on additional working conditions, the employer is required to notify the employee of such additional terms in writing within one month of commencement of the employment at the latest. Non-compliance with this requirement does not render the employment contract invalid but may result in penalties of up to EUR100 000 imposed on the employer by the relevant Work Inspectorate.

[435] Employment may be part-time or full-time and may be entered into for a fixed or indefinite term. Employment is presumed to be entered into for indefinite term unless the contract provides for a specific term.

Termination of Employment Contract

[436] Employment may be terminated by agreement, by notice, by immediate termination or by termination within the trial period. Fixed-term employment also ends upon the expiry of the period for which the employment was agreed. If employment is terminated, an employee is entitled to (i) salary until the date of termination of employment, (ii) severance payment (if applicable) and, (iii) compensation for unused vacation (if applicable).

Termination by Agreement

[437] Employment may be terminated by agreement at any time and for any reason. The agreement must be in writing. The reasons for termination must be stated in the agreement only if the employee so requests or if the employment was terminated due to organizational restructuring. The employment terminated by agreement will terminate on the agreed day.

Termination by Notice

[438] Employment may be terminated by notice given by either the employer or employee. The notice must be in writing and delivered (with proof of delivery) to the other party, or else it is invalid. Whereas the employer may only serve notice on the employee for certain reasons prescribed by the Labour Code and the notice must clearly set out the reason for the termination, the employee may serve termination notice for any reason or without stating the reason for termination.

[439] The general notice period is one month. If an employee's employment lasted at least one year, the notice period in case of termination by the employer is two months. If the employer gives notice to the employee on grounds of (i) winding-up of the employer or relocation of the employer or a part thereof and (ii) organizational changes or (iii) loss of capability to carry out the present work due to medical condition, the notice period is (a) two months, if the employment lasted between one and five years or (b) three months, if the employment lasted at least five years.

[440] If the employee terminates employment, the notice period is (i) one month in case the employment lasted less than one year and (ii) two months in case the employment lasted at least one year.

[441] The law provides protection period during which the employer cannot serve notice on the employee. This protection applies to pregnant female employees, employees on maternity or parental leave, on sickness leave, or single employees caring for a child younger than three years or employees who are called on duty or performing a public office, or employees working at night who are, according to a medical opinion, incapable of a night work during certain period.

[442] If an employer intends to terminate employment by notice (unless the employment is terminated due to violation of work discipline or unsatisfactory work performance), it must first offer to the affected employee another suitable job, if such job exists. Such alternative job must be at the place originally agreed as the place of employment, even with shorter working hours.

Immediate Termination by Employer

[443] Employer may terminate employment with immediate effect only in exceptional cases, and only for the following reasons:

(i) employee is lawfully sentenced for a wilful offence; or
(ii) employee is in a serious breach of working discipline (e.g., physically assaulted other employee, drug/alcohol abuse etc.).

[444] Employer cannot terminate employment with immediate effect with: pregnant female employee, employee on maternity leave or on parental leave, employee who is single parent taking care for a child younger than three years of age, or employee taking care for a closely related person with severe disability. Employer may terminate employment with such employees, provided that there are grounds for immediate termination, only by giving two months' notice. However, employees on maternity leave and parental leave are protected also against such form of dismissal.

Immediate Termination by Employee

[445] Employee may terminate employment with immediate effect only in exceptional cases, including serious medical reasons and failure of employer to pay salary within fifteen days from the agreed due date. In such case, the terminating employee is entitled to wage compensation totalling two average monthly salaries.

Invalid Termination

[446] The employee may challenge the termination in court within two months of the termination and, if successful, the employer would have to compensate such employee for lost income over a period of up to three years. In addition, if any breach of the Labour Code is recognized, the employer may be liable for a fine of up to EUR100 000 imposed by the relevant Inspectorate.

Information/Consultation Procedure

[447] Termination of employment by notice and immediate termination must be discussed with employee representatives, if any. The consent of such representatives is not required. The opinion of the representatives should be obtained prior to the termination otherwise the termination is invalid.

[448] In the event of a collective redundancy the notification and negotiation with employee representatives must start at least one month prior to commencement of the collective redundancy. The employer must also report to the Labour Office the outcome of these negotiations with employee representatives and the process of termination may not start earlier than one month from the report to the Labour Office.

Severance

[449] Under the Labour Code, the employer must pay to the employees whose employment is terminated by notice for (i) winding-up of the employer or relocation of the employer or a part thereof and (i) organizational changes or (iii) loss of capability to carry out the present work due to medical condition a severance payment of at least one average monthly salary, if employees are employed with the employer for more than two years and less than five years. The severance payment must be at least:

(i) two times average monthly salaries where employees are employed with the employer for more than five years and less than ten years;
(ii) three times average monthly salaries where employees are employed with the employer for more than ten years and less than twenty years;
(iii) four times average monthly salaries where employees are employed with the employer for more than twenty years.

[450] Similar severance payment is due to employees whose employment is terminated by agreement for the same reasons as listed above.

Particular Acquisition-Related Aspects

Share Transaction

[451] If an acquisition is structured as a share transaction, the identity of the employer remains unchanged. A share deal will not affect the existing employment or any of the mutual rights and obligations under existing employment contracts.

[452] In a share transaction, in general, a trade union active in the employer's undertaking has no co-decision or supervision rights in relation to the transaction, and the employer has no duty to inform the trade union (or other employee representatives) about the transaction unless it would affect employees.

Asset Transaction

[453] A different regime applies to an asset transaction where the employer changes during the transaction. In this case, all employment contracts pertaining to the acquired business transfer to the purchaser by operation of law, and no modification to the employment contract is required. As a general rule, the new employer cannot 'cherry pick' and choose which employees it takes on. An asset deal as such does not trigger the transfer of employment. Rather, this happens only if the original employer's activities are transferred.

[454] The Commercial Code stipulates that if an enterprise or a part thereof is transferred to a new owner, all employees existing at the time of the transfer and pertaining to the enterprise or the part transferred shall pass to the new owner by

operation of law. The contract must be in writing, with signatures certified by a notary public and the parties must comply with other conditions prescribed by the Slovak law. The provisions of the Commercial Code dealing with the sale of an enterprise or a part thereof are reflected in the Labour Code, which is in line with the Transfers of Undertakings Directive 2001/23/EC. If an enterprise or a part thereof is transferred to another employer, all the rights and obligations arising from the employment are transferred to the new employer. The original employer's rights and obligations towards employees whose employment was terminated before the day of the transfer remain unchanged.

[455] In general, all employment conditions and benefits, including unused annual leave, shall be unaffected by the transfer. The Labour Code does not provide for the protection period during which the employment conditions should remain unchanged with respect to the employees transferred to the new employer. However, any change of employment conditions is subject to a mutual agreement between an employer and an employee, i.e. the working conditions cannot be changed unilaterally by the employer. Should the transfer mean the material change of working conditions for the employee (e.g. change of work position or place of work) and the affected employee will not accept such change, his/her employment will be considered terminated by mutual agreement, subject to severance payment by the employer.

[456] The employer must inform in writing either the employee representatives or, if there are none, directly the employees affected by the transfer of the planned transfer. If in course of the transaction any measures are foreseen that would affect employees (e.g. re-organization or planned collective redundancy measure), negotiations must take place. The negotiations must take place or information be provided at least thirty days before the transfer is realized. Although the negotiations must take place, they do not need to lead to consent.

Non-competition

[457] An employee may carry out a business activity which could have a competing nature to the business activity of the employer only with the prior written consent of the employer. The employer may revoke such request in writing at any time. If the employee breaches this obligation, the employer may claim damages resulting from the employee's breach, or can take steps to terminate the employment on the grounds of breach of working discipline by the employee.

[458] The Labour Code provides for possibility for the employee and the employer to agree on a post-employment non-compete undertaking by the employee. The employer and employee can agree on such non-compete undertaking for a period of up to one year after the termination of employment. This option is open only to employees who, in the course of their employment, had the chance to obtain information or knowledge which is not publicly available or the use of which could cause harm to the employer. The non-compete undertaking must be proportionate to what is necessary to protect the employer and the court will have a right to amend excessive non-compete clauses. Employer is bound to provide the employee with consideration for the non-compete undertaking in the amount of at least 50% of the employee's average salary for each month of the non-compete undertaking. The parties can agree on a fair compensation to be paid to the employer in the event the employee breaches the non-compete clause. However, such compensation must not exceed the agreed consideration and, if the non-compete clause is partially fulfilled by the employee, then the compensation must be decreased accordingly.

Labour Costs

[459] The minimum wage in Slovakia as of 1 January 2019 is set at EUR520 per month. The average salary in 2018 was EUR1 013 per month and is estimated to increase to approximately EUR1 060 in 2019. Please *see also* paragraph **[387]–[425]** Taxation above describing income tax and social security implications of wages.

Pensions

[460] Pensions in the Slovak Republic are based on mandatory pension schemes to which both (employers and employees) contribute (i.e. employers do not establish separate private pension funds). Contributions to private pension schemes are completely voluntary for both employers and employees and are not subject to any specific tax benefits/relief.

Managers

[461] Under Slovak law there is no prohibition to appoint an employee to hold the position of an executive director. However if one person concurrently holds the office of an executive director and at the same time this person is also an employee with the same company, there is a risk that such employment contract could be declared invalid or ineffective provided that the duties under the employment contract cover the duties of an executive director.

[462] Foreigners (except citizens of member states of EU and the OECD) to be appointed in the management representation of the company must have a residence permit in the Slovak Republic.

[463] If an executive director breaches his/her duty to act with due care, he/she must (i) surrender to the company any profit that he/she obtained by such breach, and (ii) compensate the company for any damage. Such compensation covers both monetary damages (i.e. actual damage and lost profit) and potential non-monetary damage (e.g. a loss of reputation). If damage is caused by several directors, all such directors are liable jointly and severally.

[464] To reduce any exposure to the liabilities, we note that it is possible to arrange for directors' professional liability insurance that is customarily provided by some insurers.

Treatment of Foreign Employees

[465] Citizens of EU Member States, EEA states and Switzerland are free to work and stay in Slovakia without restriction (save for certain simple registration requirements). All other foreigners must obtain a work and residence permits in order to be allowed to stay and work in the Slovak Republic. The application for and granting of work and residence permits usually takes around ninty days and should be initiated before the foreign employee enters Slovakia at the Slovak consulate in his or her home country.

[466] Foreigners employed by a Slovak employer are automatically subject to Slovak personal income tax (for rates and more details *see* paragraph **[395]–[397]** above). Such foreigners will also usually become subject to Slovak social security system and will be obliged to pay social security contributions (detailed in paragraph **[395]–[397]** above) unless they are EU, EEA or Swiss nationals and the employment is temporary, i.e. eligible for exemption under the EU Social Security Regulation[4]. In such case, foreign employees shall remain covered by their home country social security system and get the necessary papers from their home country social insurance agency to certify this fact.

[467] Foreigners seconded to Slovakia who remain employed by their non-Slovak employer will normally not be subject to Slovak personal tax, if their stay in Slovakia is limited to less than 183 days in a year (details will depend on the relevant double tax treaty). Once this threshold is exceeded, their employer would be required to register as a 'foreign employer' in Slovakia and pay personal income tax on behalf of their Slovak-based employees.

Employee Representatives

[468] Employees may form trade unions or works councils or can be represented by 'employee trustees' as their representatives in employment matters. Alternatively, they need not be represented, in which case the employer must fulfil its certain duties (such as the duty to inform) directly to all employees.

[469] Employee representatives are essential to protect employees' interests though not as powerful as in Germany or France. In most cases, employee representatives cannot block the transaction however they can extend negotiations held between employees and employers.

[4] Regulation (EC) No 883/2004 of the European Parliament and of the Council of 29 April 2004 on the coordination of social security systems.

Trade Unions

[470] Trade unions operate in the Slovak Republic on the following basic principles:

(i) trade unions may be established irrespective of the will of the employer or state authorities; and
(ii) it is forbidden to restrict in any way the establishment of trade unions or membership in a trade union, or for an employer to favour any trade union in a particular company or industry.

[471] Trade unions operate at a company level, but can also form sizeable organizations (called confederations) operating nationwide.

Works Councils and Employee Trustee

[472] A works council represents all employees of an employer and may operate with employers employing at least fifty employees. The works council may coexist together with trade unions.

[473] The employer who employs less than fifty employees but more than five employees may establish the position of the 'employee trustee'. The rights and duties of the employee trustee are the same as those of the works council.

[474] On a written request of at least 10% of its employees, the employer must organize elections to works council. The works council is duly elected only if more than 30% of all employees who have the right to vote participate in the election.

[475] The employee trustee is elected directly by a secret ballot by absolute majority of employees present at the voting. Both works council and employee trustee are elected for the term of four years.

[476] Works councils always operate within one employer. Unlike trade unions, they cannot create structures covering more than one employer.

[477] A works council operates as mediator between the employer and its employees. It has fewer powers than a trade union. The works council acts for employees in the exercise of their right to information and consultations. Works councils are not legal entities (i.e., they have no legal capacity). Also, works councils do not have a right to carry out collective bargaining or to execute collective agreements, and therefore cannot employ extreme measures, such as strikes, to resolve collective disputes. However, if there is no trade union within the employer, work council and work trustee can enter into agreements with the employer, governing the conditions of work, including salary, to the same extent as may be agreed in a collective agreement.

Collective Bargaining and Collective Agreements

[478] Trade unions are exclusive representatives of employees in collective bargaining and in the process of conclusion of collective agreements. Trade unions execute these agreements on behalf of all employees at the company level (company collective agreements) or at the industry level (so-called 'higher-level collective agreements').

[479] Higher-level collective agreements are binding on all employees and employers in the industry/business in question and will cover also all businesses or industries that are named in a generally binding act of the Ministry of Labour of the Slovak Republic.

[480] If there are several trade unions operating on employer's premises, the employer will collectively bargain with all of them that cooperate with each other. If they do not cooperate with each other, the employer may enter into a collective agreement with that trade union that has the largest number of members or with other trade unions that, in aggregate, have more members than the largest trade union.

Right to Information

[481] Employers must provide certain information to employees or works councils (such as details about prospective development of employment and any contemplated structural changes in the company).

[482] 'Right to information' means the provision of the necessary information by the employer to employee representatives. The employer must provide information sufficiently in advance and in a suitable manner so that employees can consider them and give their position before any measure is implemented.

[483] Where there are active trade unions in companies, employers must provide them even more information. For example, employers must inform trade unions on an ongoing basis about any expected changes to wage/salary levels, average wage, company's economic and financial situation, working conditions and structure of the workforce. The employer's obligation to provide information does not affect its power to decide in its own discretion.

Right to Consultation

[484] The employer must bring certain issues forward to the employee representatives for consultation before any decision is taken. The decision remains exclusively with the employer but failure to consult with the employee representatives may be penalized by the Work Inspectorate.

[485] Right to consultation refers to consultation between the employer and employee representatives, the exchange of views and explanations with the aim to reach an agreement. The employer is required to arrange for a consultation to take place sufficiently in advance and in an appropriate manner so that employees could express their views and so that these views could be taken into account before the employer implements the measure. Employees have the right to a reasoned response to their views. The employees have the right to demand sufficient information and explanations before the measure is implemented.

[486] The Slovak law provides a non-exhaustive list of topics the employer must consult with employee representatives. For example, employer must consult the structure and anticipated development of employment, major social policy issues, measures for improving hygiene in the workplace, decisions that may trigger changes in organization of labour, organizational changes (merger, demerger or change of legal form) and all measures aimed at avoidance of accidents and occupational diseases, including protection of health of employees.

Right to Decide Jointly

[487] Another power enjoyed by the trade unions is the right to decide on certain matters jointly with the employer, such as adoption of the code of conduct or the drawing of paid holiday. The Slovak law provides an exhaustive list of these matters, which cannot be expanded in the collective agreement.

[488] Joint decision-making means that certain measures proposed by the employer may only be introduced with the prior consent of the trade unions. Employers must obtain a prior consent of the trade union to termination (including immediate) of employment with an employee who is a trade union member, member of works council or an employee trustee during his or her term of office and one year after its expiry. However, such employee may agree to the termination.

Right to Decide Independently

[489] In certain situations described in law, trade unions make decisions themselves. Such decisions are binding on third parties.

[490] Trade unions decide independently on issues such as those related to their establishment, internal structure, activities, assets, membership fees and potential employment of staff for their own needs. Against its employees, a trade union acts as employer and remunerates them.

[491] In certain cases (expressly set out by law) such as matters of health protection and safety of operations, trade unions may request the employer to stop the work. However, they may do so only if there is an imminent threat to life or health.

Right of Supervision

[492] Trade unions may supervise how the employer observes all labour-related provisions, including wages, and the obligations resulting from a collective agreement.

[493] When conducting supervision in matters of health and safety in the workplace, trade union bodies may also access workplace, require necessary information and supporting documents, put forward proposals improving working conditions, propose measure against executive employees who have breached their duties, and request information on measures resulting from inspection.

ACCOUNTING TREATMENT

Accounting Obligations

[494] Slovak businesses (Slovak-based companies or branch offices of foreign companies) are obliged to maintain double-entry books and to prepare annual financial statements in accordance with Slovak Accounting Standards.

[495] In addition, several types of (mainly regulated) entities must maintain books and prepare annual financial statements in accordance with IFRS. These include banks, insurance companies, collective investment companies, pension insurance companies and several other regulated businesses. IFRS must also be used by 'large' businesses. Large businesses are understood to be companies which meet at least two of the following three criteria for at least two consecutive years:

(i) total assets exceed EUR170 m;
(ii) total turnover exceeds EUR170 m; and/or
(iii) total number of employees exceeds 2 000.

[496] Other businesses that issued securities registered in a regulated securities market in one of the EU Member States may choose IFRS instead of Slovak Accounting Standards.

[497] The Slovak Accounting Standards are generally comparable to IFRS, although differences exist in certain areas.

[498] Businesses can elect any twelve-month period to be their fiscal year.

Acquisitions

Acquisition of Assets

[499] If there are individual prices set for assets in a purchase agreement, the buyer will always record the assets on its balance sheet at the agreed price plus any related acquisition costs.

[500] If there is only one lump-sum price defined in the purchase agreement, the total price for individual assets is set subject to an appraiser's report or a purchaser's reasonable judgment.

[501] In either case, no separate goodwill is recorded by the purchaser on its balance sheet – it is always reflected in the value of acquired assets and depreciated on the basis of useful life of those assets. Each time the purchaser prepares financial statements (typically, on annual basis), it should perform impairment review and create provisions for any reductions in the value of assets recorded on its balance sheet.

[502] The seller recognizes the profit on its P&L account in the accounting period in which the assets (control over the assets) are effectively handed over to the purchaser. This is usually closing of the transaction, but in some circumstances it can be a different date and may be separated from transfer of legal title to assets.

Acquisition of Shares

[503] The buyer records the shares at their acquisition price, which is, in principle, the agreed purchase price plus any related acquisition costs. Goodwill is thus reflected in the purchase price for shares and as such cannot be depreciated. Similarly to the assets acquisition, the market value of acquired shares should be regularly reviewed by the purchaser and provisions should be created in annual financial statements to reflect any reduction in the market value of acquired shares.

[504] Profits/losses of the acquired target company are consolidated with the accounts of the purchaser immediately after closing, i.e. after the purchaser acquires effective control of the target.

[505] Similarly to asset sale, the seller recognizes the profit on its P&L account in the accounting period in which the shares are effectively handed over to the purchaser and the seller loses the ability to benefit from their ownership.

Transformations

Merger/De-merger

[506] A transformation takes effect, for accounting purposes, on its Effective Date as agreed in the relevant transformation documents, such as in the merger project or merger agreement (the 'Effective Date'). The Effective Date is usually agreed to be the date when real control is acquired by the successor company(ies) over the business of the predecessor company(ies), but this can also be a different date and can be agreed relatively freely by the participants.

[507] The companies involved are required to prepare extraordinary financial statements as at a date preceding the Effective Date. In all transformations, assets and liabilities of the dissolved company must be re-valued to reflect their real market value. The corresponding goodwill is not depreciated, but instead increases or reduces the successor's equity (tax effect of such revaluation is described in paragraph 0**[420]**–**[423]** above).

[508] The successor company is required to prepare an opening balance sheet as at the Effective Date. The successor company takes over (i) valuation difference to acquired property, (ii) goodwill from previous transformations, (iii) adjustments to individual categories of assets, (iv) temporary assets and liabilities, and (v) reserves recorded by the dissolved company only if the agreement between the companies (such as merger project or de-merger project) provides for this.

[509] Special attention should be paid to mergers where one of the companies involved in a merger holds an ownership interest or shares in another company involved in the merger (such as in a situation of merger of a parent and its subsidiary). The value of eliminated shares issued by a dissolved company reduces the equity in the opening balance sheet of the successor company. If the company holding eliminated shares is highly leveraged, the successor company may report negative equity as a result of the merger. This might have various indirect legal consequences, for example, in terms of bankruptcy tests.

Transformation of the Legal Form

[510] A transformation of a company's legal form has no effect on the valuation of the company's assets on its balance sheet.

[511] Where a limited liability company, a joint-stock company or a cooperative is transferred into a general partnership or a limited partnership or vice versa, the company is required to close its books and prepare extraordinary financial statements.

FUTURE DEVELOPMENTS

[512] At the time of writing, there are no anticipated legislation changes that would significantly change existing M&A trends and practices in Slovakia. To the contrary, the legal environment relevant for M&A in Slovakia is becoming more stable over recent years.

Made in the USA
Monee, IL
18 October 2026

66041398R10057